a+t

Caruso St John Architects
Javier Mozas
Edited by Aurora Fernández Per

THE OFFICE ON THE GRASS
THE EVOLUTION OF THE WORKPLACE

"They left their desk and, after a hundred yards of glass hallway, walked through high double doors into the open air. They climbed a wide stairway. "We just finished the roof deck", he said. "I think you'll like it." When they reached the top of the stairs, the view was spectacular. The roof overlooked most of the campus, the surrounding city of San Vincenzo and the bay beyond."

Dave Eggers.
The Circle, 2013.

a+t

Title
The Office on the Grass

Subtitle
The Evolution of the Workplace

Authors
Caruso St John Architects
Javier Mozas
Aurora Fernández Per

Editor English-language version
Ken Mortimer

Cover
Facebook headquarters roof garden. Menlo Park, Ca.
Drawing by Javier Mozas.

ISBN
978-84-697-5535-8

Layout and production
Aurora Fernández Per
Delia Argote

Managing
Idoia Esteban

Communication and Press
Patricia García

Printing
Gráficas Irudi s.l.
VI 596-2017
Vitoria-Gasteiz, 2017

Published by a+t architecture publishers
© Edition: a+t architecture publishers
© Texts, drawings and photos: their authors

No part of this publication, including the cover, may be reproduced or transmitted without the express authorization in writing of the publisher.

a+t architecture publishers
Calle General Álava, 15.
01005 Vitoria-Gasteiz. Spain.

www.aplust.net

CONTENTS

A Short History of the Development of the Office
Explained in Terms of the Economic
and Social Context of the Last 100 Years.
CARUSO ST JOHN ARCHITECTS
8-41

The Liquid Nature of Workspace
Sources of Inspiration
JAVIER MOZAS
42-115

Changing Roles
JAVIER MOZAS
116-121

Glossary
123-147

Timeline
148-158

Bibliography
159

A Short History of the Development of the Office Explained in Terms of the Economic and Social Context of the Last 100 Years

CARUSO ST JOHN ARCHITECTS

John Soane. The Four Percent
office, Bank of England.
London, 1818-1823.

THE ORIGIN OF THE OFFICE

The office has existed in one form or another throughout history as an administrative adjunct to the centralised power of the state. The Palazzo Uffizi in Florence of the Medici or the Bank of England are notable examples.

The first commercial offices appeared in the northern industrial cities of the United States in the late nineteenth Century. With the invention of the telegraph and telephone, offices could be situated away from the home or factory and control could be retained over production and distribution to distant markets. New technologies such as electric lighting, the typewriter and the use of calculating machines allowed large amounts of information to be accumulated and processed faster and more efficiently than before. The concentration of wealth in the new corporations required an ever-greater proportion of an increasingly literate population to work in the 'white collar factories'.

In Chicago, the mid-western hub of the American rail network, technologies such as the steel frame and elevator enabled office buildings to be constructed higher than previously possible to generate maximum income from the site. These were the first speculative office buildings and generally followed the traditional layout of separate rooms opening into corridors. The floor plan would then be stacked to generate the greatest income from the site —this profit-driven logic came to define the skylines of Chicago and New York by the early twentieth Century.

The American architect Louis Sullivan was a pioneer in his study of the formal articulation of the tall commercial building or 'skyscraper'; his delicate naturalist ornamentation and bold forms expressed his own mystical vision of a new and vital democracy based on industrialisation.

THE OFFICE ON THE GRASS

Louis Sullivan.
Wainwright Building.
St. Louis, Mo., 1890-1891.

THE TAYLORIST OPEN PLAN
The production-line nature of much American office work in the early twentieth Century resulted in the work-pool arrangement of clerical workers lined up in rows in large rooms. Mail-order firms, insurance companies and government agencies followed the Taylorist principles of splitting tasks into specific repetitive acts. These regimented spaces enabled an uninterrupted flow of work and close visual supervision by managers often having their own offices. The other economic gain derived from such a layout was that more desks could be fitted into open areas than cellular rooms.

It was Sullivan's ex-employee, Frank Lloyd Wright, who first attempted to temper these harsh conditions. He had by this time developed his own visionary position informed by the social ideals of William Morris and the Arts and Crafts movement and a concern for the individual's place in industrial society.

The Larkin Administration Building of 1903-1905 in Buffalo, New York, was designed by Wright for a mail order soap company of 1,800 workers, and can be considered the first purpose-designed environment for a specific organisation. The cliff-like brick building was innovative in plan with all service spaces pulled to the corners leaving a large open space at the centre. To keep the interior space free from the pollution of passing New York trains the building was hermetically sealed and provided with one of the first primitive air-conditioning systems. Managers and clerks, many of them women, worked together in a single large space of galleries surrounding a central top-lit court, processing more than 5,000 orders per day. Views out were limited to glimpses of the sky creating an introverted sense of the company as a family dedicated to the 'sacrament of work', as emphasised by the salutary inscriptions on the galleries. Wright's attention to detail extended to the design of the steel furniture, the first 'system' furniture and the built-in cabinets that lined the walls.

THE OFFICE ON THE GRASS

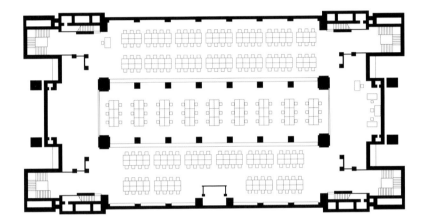

Frank Lloyd Wright.
Larkin Administration
Building.
Buffalo, N. Y., 1903-1905.

EUROPEAN MODERN MOVEMENT

The scale and innovations of American examples were emulated to a limited extent in the more traditional countries of Europe. The Taylorist office started to appear at a smaller scale just as miniature skyscrapers were beginning to be built in some European cities. Many artists and architects involved in the European modern movement admired the modern and rationalist American examples but lacked the resources or opportunity to carry out their ideas. Mies van der Rohe's visionary conceptual projects of the 1920s for crystalline glass towers would find fruition many years later in the corporate architecture of post-war America. In his more rationalist 'concrete office building' project, stacked concrete trays holding work areas were lit by continuous ribbon windows. As in Wright's office buildings, the occupants have no view out to the surroundings as the windows were above head height, the space below the window being used for storage cabinets.

Le Corbusier's glass curtain wall project for government offices in Brazil of 1936 expressed a more open ideal; the literal and organisational transparency of a modern democratic state.

THE OFFICE ON THE GRASS

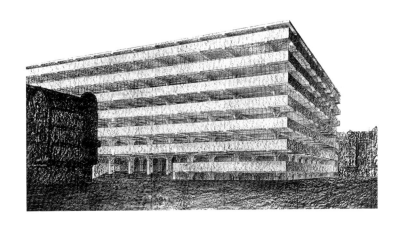

Mies van der Rohe.
Concrete Office Building.
Berlin, 1922.

Le Corbusier.
Offices of the Ministry for
National Education and Health.
Rio de Janeiro, 1936.

STREAMLINED OFFICE PLAN

Having developed solutions to the problems of organisation and manufacture, the 1930s saw American companies becoming interested in more efficient working environments and buildings that could express their corporate image.

Wright extended his idea of the company as an organic social entity with the construction of the Johnson Wax building in 1937-1939. As with the Larkin building, workers were isolated from the unsympathetic industrial surroundings within a great space supported by slender mushroom columns and lit from above. The great work room, with its rich spaces, warm, radiant materials and forms were intended to compensate for the lack of view and contact with the outside world.

The *St Louis Dispatch* reported in 1937 during construction:
'The 250 workers will occupy a single great room, only those machines which are noisy being segregated, and cork ceilings will absorb the sound rising from the heated rubber floor, blend it into a placid hum.'

The Johnson Wax building created a sensation when it opened and the building is still in use by the same company today, admired as one of the masterpieces of 1930s architecture.

The organisation of this cleaning materials company was again based on Taylorist principles and a clear and rigid hierarchy. Orders would be processed across the main work floor with managers overlooking from the mezzanine. Company executives were in their own offices on the roof of the building with a bridge connection to the research laboratories.

Within the hierarchical structure of the company the paternalistic nature of the company is manifest in the facilities for its unionised workers such as a theatre. The success of the building was proved by the extra time that employees chose to spend in the building.

THE OFFICE ON THE GRASS

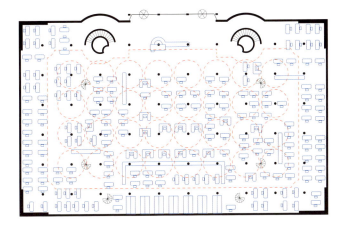

Frank Lloyd Wright. Johnson-
Wax Administration Building.
Racine, Wi., 1937-1939.

50'S CORPORATE AMERICA

In the 1950s the steel and glass architecture of the international modern movement was adopted as the new image of corporate America. The Lever House of 1952 designed by Skidmore Owings and Merrill was the first project to offer the modernist image of efficiency and standardisation to a corporate client.

In the 1950s and 60s a number of these hermetically sealed 'glass boxes' were built in New York and expressed the city's commercial and cultural dominance. The large sculpture on the plaza and the elegant high modernist interior, epitomised by interior designers such as the Knoll planning Unit, became the new international language of business and success.

With the widespread use of air-conditioning and fluorescent lighting, these new high-rise buildings could have highly efficient deep and open floors. There was now no longer an imperative to have natural lighting, whether from windows or skylights, or to be near an opening window for ventilation. The suspended ceiling took over these functions, containing lighting and air distribution. The office had successfully become fully autonomous from the exterior environment.

This formula was influential worldwide. The 1967 film *Playtime* by Jacques Tati pokes fun at this idea of the Modernist city, following a group of American tourists touring a steel and glass metropolis looking for the 'real' Paris.

The Chase Manhattan Bank of 1961 illustrates the essentially hierarchical nature of American business, where administrative and clerical staff still worked in open pools, managers in partitioned offices and executives in the luxury of the sixtieth floor.

THE OFFICE ON THE GRASS

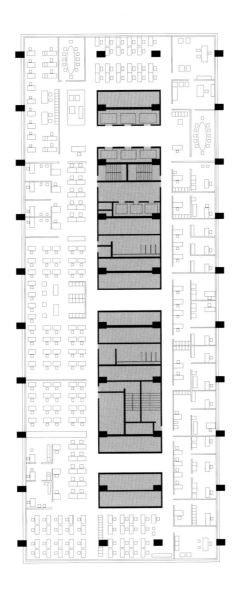

Skidmore Owings and
Merrill.
Chase-Manhattan Bank.
New York, 1961.

OFFICE-LANDSCAPE

In the 1950s in Germany, the Quickborner team of management consultants developed the radical office layout idea of *Bürolandschaft* or 'office-landscape'. This consisted of free and open plans of furniture scattered in large, structurally undivided spaces with mechanically controlled environments. Unlike the American open plan, strategic use of partitions and large plants created some degree of differentiation and privacy. The use of carpets and ceiling absorbing panels tempered the noise of a large office to some degree.

Derived from organisational theory, the rationale of *Bürolandschaft* was based on a more complex scientific 'model' of 'human relations' rather than Taylorism. For the first time the widely diverse nature of kinds of office work was recognised and the Quickborner team devised criteria for fitting a particular kind of office to a specific type of layout.

The Social Democratic nature of post-war government in many Northern European countries fostered a more egalitarian management approach. The Quickborner team encouraged all ranks of company staff to sit together on one open floor in an attempt to create a non-hierarchical environment that increased communication between people and allowed for future flexibility.

Bürolandschaft enjoyed a brief period of popularity in Europe, especially in Germany, and was picked up in some British offices by the end of the 1960s. Furniture systems such as Herman Miller Action Furniture was developed to adapt the desk to this new office environment and respond to concerns about noise and privacy. Such furniture began to accumulate built-in partitions and storage in an attempt to confer the status of small rooms to each desk in an open plan, in this way undermining the original open and charmingly random quality of *Bürolandschaft*.

THE OFFICE ON THE GRASS

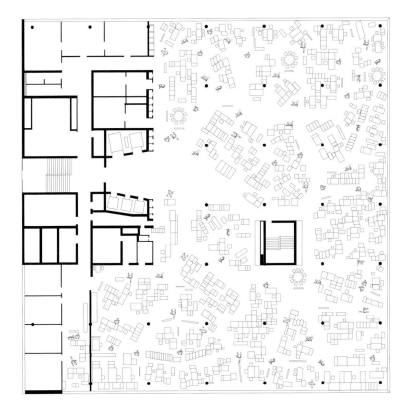

**Walter Henn.
Osram Offices.
Munich, 1963.**

STRUCTURALIST OFFICE
In the 1950s the supremacy of the Modernist model of the functional city had started to be criticised and certain designers looked to the patterns and human associations of the traditional city and archetypal forms of other cultures such as the North African Kasbah. The Dutch architect Herman Hertzberger developed a kind of structuralist architecture influenced by the ethnic anthropologist Claude Lévi-Strauss. Hertzberger's Centraal Beheer insurance company project –built in Apeldoorn, Holland in 1970-1973– is a kind of 'workers' village' designed so that the occupants 'would have the feeling of being part of a working community without being lost in the crowd'. The building is a deep spatial matrix of concrete and blockwork arranged on a tartan grid. Platforms separated by light wells enable light to filter down into the centre of the plan. The unfinished quality of the materials and the repetitive nature of these small platforms allowed them to be appropriated by small groups of 8-10 people who were encouraged to personalise and decorate the space. The company actively encouraged a sense of the family to enter the office and many workers actually brought pieces of furniture and members of their family from home into work.

The collective 'human scale' language of the architecture however did not extend to providing large representative public spaces for the organisation and its labyrinthine quality meant that it was very easy to become lost inside the deep plan. The Centraal Beheer is most notable for its success in empowering the individual and reflected a general trend in Europe of a steadily increasing status for the office worker. Compared to previous examples the amount of space per person is very high as there is so much circulation; it is certainly much less efficient that any form of open plan. The driving force behind the building is the Company's decision to place the human resource of their staff above questions of efficiency or economy.

THE OFFICE ON THE GRASS

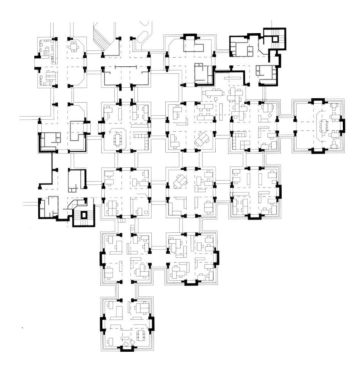

Herman Hertzberger.
Centraal Beheer.
Apeldoorn, 1970-1973.

EURO STAKEHOLDER OFFICE

The rejection of *Bürolandschaft* in Continental Europe more or less corresponded with the Economic crisis of 1973 triggered by increases in energy costs. Deep expanses of air-conditioned and artificially lit office space seemed less sustainable and the difficulty some found in adapting to open office environments resulted in its fall from fashion.

The increasing involvement of the employee in corporate decision-making resulted in workers councils that became influential in the design of the working environment. Countries such as Sweden, Germany and The Netherlands adopted regulations that governed space standards per employee and demanded access to views, daylight and openable windows. Personal control of the environment was seen to be a very important factor in the well being of the worker. As office workers became more enfranchised this control extended to the actual organisation and ownership of companies, many opting to give their employees the opportunity to become stakeholders.

The result of this development is the model that remains dominant today for Continental European offices. New office buildings follow the general pattern of narrow buildings of cellular offices arranged along a central corridor. The ambition for each employee to work in their own office or amongst a small group was the new formula that seemed to contradict all the claims of *Bürolandschaft*. European companies are generally owner-occupiers and their buildings are purpose built for their needs. The result of well meaning but inflexible regulations is that many office environments do not express the culture of their organisations in a positive and integrated way and many monotonous cellular offices are the result.

Recent attempts to create a more public realm in the European office have taken the form of cellular offices with public 'streets' with cafes and relaxation areas such as the Stockholm SAS building by Niels Torp of 1987. The 'combi-office' invented by the Swedish practice Tengbom combines cellular offices on the exterior of a building with a common space for employees and services in the centre.

There is now also a strong ecological and sustainability agenda in the production of new office buildings on the continent, as an extension of the socially responsible ethos of the stakeholder model.

THE OFFICE ON THE GRASS

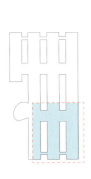

Steidle and Kiessler. Gruner & Jahr. Hamburg, 1985.

US/UK SHAREHOLDER OFFICE

In Britain and America a more hierarchical corporate culture has resulted in a different response to *Bürolandschaft*. The space efficiency and perceived communication benefits of the open plan were retained but the underlying ethos has remained that of the Taylorist office. Many offices have a mixture of cellular offices for senior managers and open plan space for other workers. Both the developers who build these buildings and the companies that occupy them are ultimately responsible to the shareholder rather than to the employee.

Significantly higher rents in London than in other European cities and relatively few regulations regarding space standards in offices has resulted in deeper and more open office plans. The use of compact and efficient American-style open plans developed into the large dealing floors that became popular with financial services firms following the deregulation of the stock market in 1986. A great deal of interaction and urgency characterises this type of work. Deep raised floors were needed to accommodate the large amounts of services needed for the widespread use of the computer in such expansive spaces. Broadgate by Arup Associates in the City of London, 1987, is a model development of this type. Large scale developments in Canary Wharf from the 1990s follow more closely the American model of the office.

In the UK office buildings are often designed as empty shells that only generally anticipate the organisations that will occupy the future building. It is usual for companies to rent rather than buy their space and therefore building developers dominate the office market. Offices are also often set up in old buildings such as warehouses that may not have been purpose-designed, but offer generously scaled and flexible spaces.

Another trend that became widespread in Britain and America is the out-of-town business park, with its cheaper rents than central city locations. In the UK this phenomenon is often driven by the logic of the cost-cutting management consultant and the increasing mobility of day-to-day office work. Many of these developments have used the increased amount of open space to build shallower plan offices with more contact with the outside. The deep, artificially lit and air-conditioned, plan has been linked to 'sick building syndrome' and higher employee absenteeism and dissatisfaction.

THE OFFICE ON THE GRASS

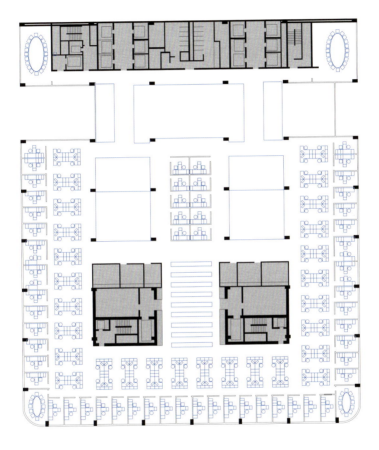

Foster and Partners. Citibank
Headquarters, Canary Wharf.
London, 1996-2000.

THE VIRTUAL OFFICE

The influences of branding and information technology have had the greatest effect on recent developments of the office. The widespread use of the Internet, laptops and mobile phones has created a much more fluid situation. Work could become more mobile and move from the office to the café or the home. The cost savings of teleworking and outsourcing could not be ignored by companies facing new demands to remain competitive in the globalised markets of the 1990s.

The British Telecom office in Stockley Park, on the M25 near Heathrow airport, is an open plan business park building occupied as part of their 'Workstyle 2000' initiative. This branded process was created to smooth the transition from being a public utility to a privatised company competing in a global telecommunications market. British Telecom took the opportunity to change the working culture of their organisation, selling off properties in inner city areas and moving to the outskirts and regional hubs. At Stockley Park staff –mostly managers previously accustomed to cellular offices in West London– now travel to work by car and spend a maximum of three days a week in the office –the remainder spent with clients or working from home.

In the actual office environment, designed to enable 'hot-desking' and more team-based working, the unimaginative and regularized open plan has made it difficult for people to identify or feel at home and departmental groupings are unclear. Fast-track construction has made it difficult to consult with the future users, so while the result may be increased efficiency and profits for the company it actually illustrates only the most up-to date version of the Taylorist attitudes that have dominated the office throughout its history. The new territories of the motorway, airport and trading estate –or the non-place– celebrated in the novels of James Graham Ballard are now the familiar everyday working experience for many office workers.

THE OFFICE ON THE GRASS

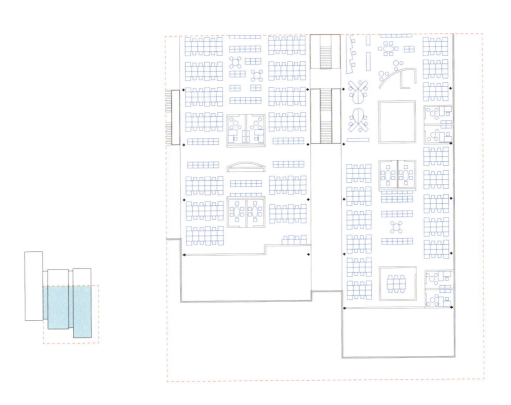

DEGW (fit-out) British Telecom offices. Stockley Park, 1996.

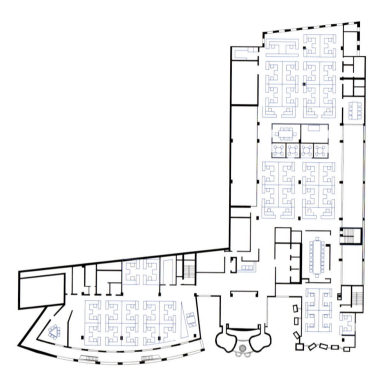

Clive Wilkinson Architects.
TBWA/Chiat/Day offices.
Los Angeles, 1998.

THE CASUAL OFFICE

A parallel trend in office design is the casual office pioneered by Silicon Valley software firms in the eighties, which encourages highly personalised workspaces suited to long hours spent programming. The 'dress code' of such an office became much more relaxed than a conventional office. As this approach becomes more widespread, especially in creative industries in fashionable central city locations, many have started to become open 24 hours to enable more flexible working patterns. Clearly these offices are the environments where design and creative thinking are developing new ideas that can make the office a more inspiring place.

Office Paradigms

Different possibilities of plan layout inspired by examples from outside the office.

Texts and drawings by Caruso St John Architects

The Library

The library is arranged like an onion: on the outside are quiet working areas, peeling away this layer, a ring of circulation lies within. Deeper inside an inner layer of services and book stacks surrounds a central space –the focus of the library.

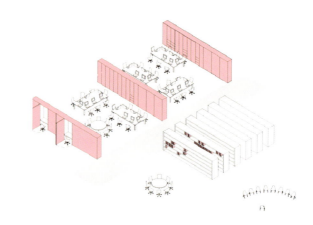

Louis I. Kahn.
Philip Exeter Academy Library.
Exeter N. H., 1965-1971.

THE OFFICE ON THE GRASS

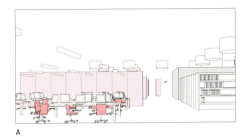

A

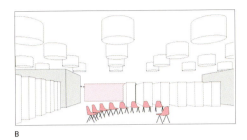

B

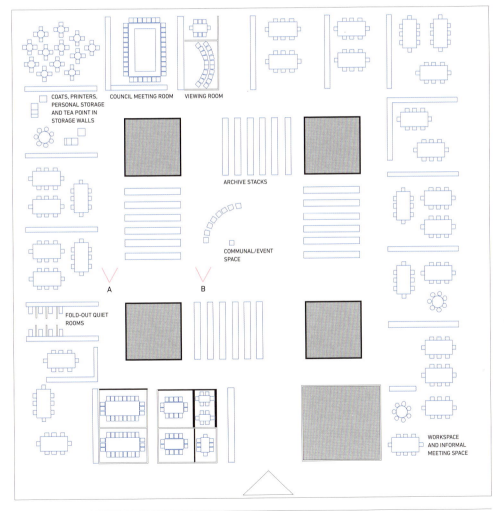

COATS, PRINTERS, PERSONAL STORAGE AND TEA POINT IN STORAGE WALLS

COUNCIL MEETING ROOM

VIEWING ROOM

ARCHIVE STACKS

COMMUNAL/EVENT SPACE

FOLD-OUT QUIET ROOMS

WORKSPACE AND INFORMAL MEETING SPACE

Archipelago

An informal arrangement of islands is surrounded by a sea of different conditions: wide sounds, narrower channels and more sheltered bays and inlets.

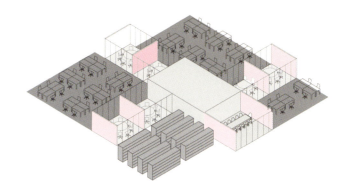

Archipelago in Stockholm.

THE OFFICE ON THE GRASS

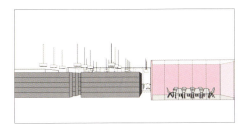

A

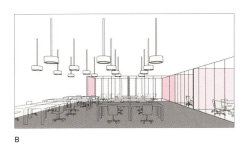

B

WORKSPACE
SERVICE AREA
TEAM MEETING AREA
ARCHIVE STACKS
FORMAL MEETING ROOM

Great Rooms

Each room has a different atmosphere and concentrates a specific and focused community. The spaces between are free flowing around and between the rooms: here there is a more diffused and informal atmosphere.

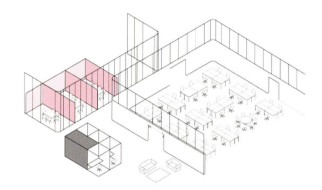

Louis Le Vau, Jules Hardouin-Mansart, Robert de Cotte, Jacques V Gabriel, Ange-Jacques Gabriel. Chateau de Versailles, 1623-1682.

THE OFFICE ON THE GRASS

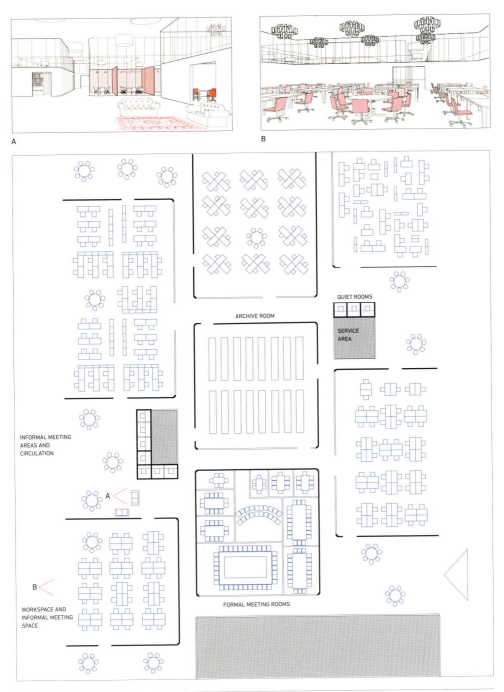

Fields

Territories or fields are established by boundary lines –in each one a different kind of cultivation occurs. They are distinct but it is possible to cross from one into another.

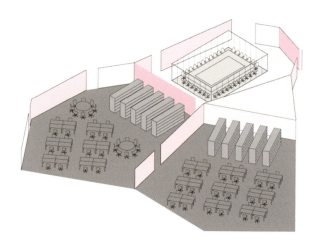

THE OFFICE ON THE GRASS

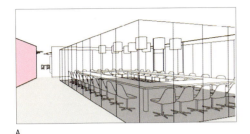

A

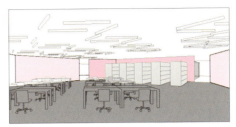

B

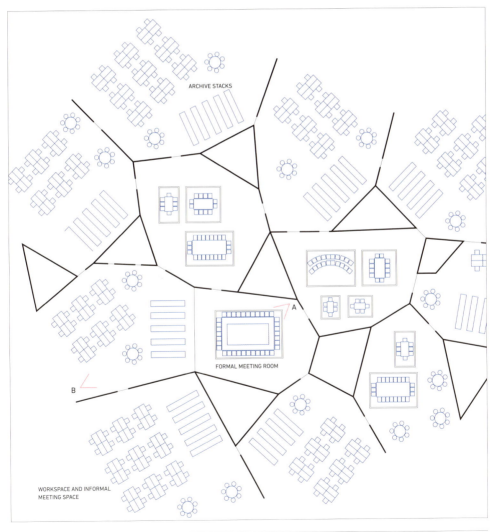

ARCHIVE STACKS

A

FORMAL MEETING ROOM

B

WORKSPACE AND INFORMAL
MEETING SPACE

City Grid

A grid of continuous repeated units that accomodates difference and specific moments within a homogenous pattern.

Santo Domingo, 1671.

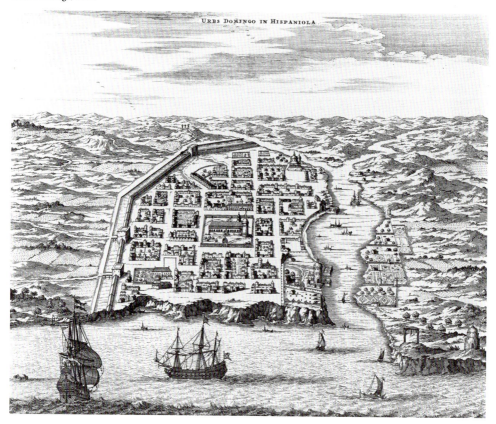

THE OFFICE ON THE GRASS

A

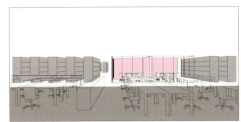

B

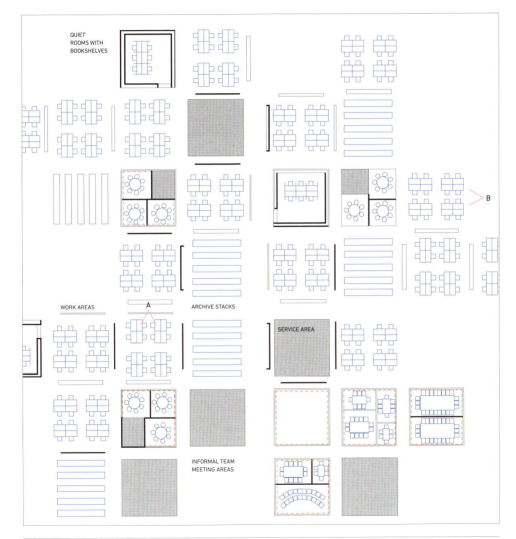

QUIET ROOMS WITH BOOKSHELVES

WORK AREAS

A

ARCHIVE STACKS

SERVICE AREA

B

INFORMAL TEAM MEETING AREAS

The Liquid Nature of Workspace

JAVIER MOZAS

Work is work. It's hard and it was done to earn your bread. The imposition laid out in Genesis stated this was with the sweat of your brow. That was until the connection between work and capital was discovered. These are different times. There exist thrilling paradises which disguise the true essence of work and blur this function in the mixture of activities, with no long-term solution, which everyday routine is turning into. Leisure (the Latin term *otium*) and its antithesis, business (*nec-otium*, what is not *otium*), blend together in a continuous pretence which spreads beyond the workplace.

The technological revolution increased productivity with the presence of machines and robots in production lines and the workplace was stripped of any discomfort and dependence on weather conditions. The ties with a physical location were broken and work began to merge with other human activities such as living, learning and socializing which had their own spheres of development.

We are witnessing the abolition of the standard scheduling of everyday activities encouraged by the multi-tasking options provided by mobile devices. We can do anything at any time in any place. Daily life is liquefied in a continuous undefined shell with no specific space or time.

1. Zygmunt Bauman. *The Liquid Modernity*. Polity Press, 2000 p. 194.

"The passage from heavy to light capitalism and from solid to fluid or liquefied modernity constitutes the framework in which the history of the labour movement has been inscribed."

ZYGMUNT BAUMAN.[1]

Wallpaper based on the 'global spirit of a modern digital workspace' that recreates the landscape work of the Living Office Series.

BETTER TOGETHER

Just as in the Middle Ages associations were set up to defend the rights of tradespeople, self-employed working[2] has been strengthening its position against that enjoyed by the corporate employee. New Mutualism[3] is one of the recent approaches adopted by freelancers and its principles can be summed up as follows: let's do it together if we can't do it on our own, let's do it ourselves, and let's always do it driven by a social mission. This is the essence of this new movement which puts its trust in the power of the community.

As the Millennials or Y Generation –young adolescents who became adults at the turn of the century– have joined the job market, cracks have formed in the monolithic environment that is the corporate office. This generation is noted for its being technology-dependent, more open, better-educated and most of all for its desire to participate and collaborate.[4] It takes ownership of the philosophy 'better together' endorsed by shared offices or coworking centres.

Agora Collective[5] is a space which has a magic formula combining three magnetic ingredients: work, art and food. It is located in a five-storey brick building in the Neukölln area of Berlin. In theory, it is a place for professionals from all fields. However, the main focus is on creative work. There is a non-stop stream of activities: encounters, talks by artists, workshops, exhibitions, shows, dinners, pop-ups, meet-ups... The ideological lines of these work spaces deal with the collaborative economy, lateral thinking and they are well aware that they are facing the challenges of their working lives on the basis of seemingly illogical resources such as chance or provocation. The search for personal relationships is not justified by the need for physical contact. Instead it is associated with scientific or literary terms such as: creative collisions, cross-pollination and serendipitous encounters.

Nevertheless, the need for an enclosed space still exists when privacy is a priority. Some coworking centres[6] are becoming farms of glazed pods with access which is either individual or shared by a limited number of individuals who choose to reject the social element of the shared space. New layouts have been established based on a real demand taken into consideration by the companies which manage these spaces in their aim for a good return on investment.

---

2. Steven F. Hipple. "About 1 in 9 workers was self-employed in 2009". Self-employment in the United States. *Monthly Labor Review*. September 2010. http://www.bls.gov/opub/mlr/2010/09/art2full.pdf
3. Sara Horowitz. *What is New Mutualism?* Freelancers Union. Freelancers Broadcasting Network. Dispatches. https://www.freelancersunion.org/blog/dispatches/2013/11/05/what-new-mutualism/
4. *Millennials. A portrait of Generation Next. Confident. Connected. Open to Change.* Pew Research Center, 2010. http://www.pewsocialtrends.org/files/2010/10/millennials-confident-connected-open-to-change.pdf
5. http://agoracollective.org/
6. WeWork. New York. https://www.http://www.wework.com/

THE OFFICE ON THE GRASS

WHY DO YOU FREELANCE? % is how many respondents said these considerations were "important or extremely important" to them

BE FLEXIBLE	CONTROL MY OWN SCHEDULE	BE MY OWN BOSS	DO WHAT I LOVE	BALANCE MY OWN WORK & LIFE
78%	**77%**	**75%**	**75%**	**62%**

SARA HOROWITZ, FREELANCERS UNION.

Shared space in Berlin Agora Collective.

AGORA COLLECTIVE

Private offices with glass partitions at WeWork, New York.

WEWORK

THE FUN OFFICE

In the 1990s, outside working hours employees used to carry out non-productive activities which had no relation to their work. It was a time when there was a clear distinction between business time and leisure time. There was a clearer division between the different functions. Nowadays, since information technology has managed to become ubiquitous and social media is 24/7, the working day is latent even during rest times. Production never stops albeit it has now taken on a different form. The upshot of this stretched schedule is more relaxed production combined with other lighter activities to ease up the long working day. Productivity has been reduced in terms of density.

Fun and games have helped to overcome obstacles and activate those creative thoughts which are the very basis of innovation.[7] Googleplex, the Google HQ in Mountain View, California, is a result of refurbishment work on the building inherited from Silicon Graphics in 2003, to which Clive Wilkinson Architects applied the 'campus office' concept in 2005. The architectural solution is based on a set of participatory ideas, developed in the mid-1990s in small coworking centres in the San Francisco metropolitan area, which recreated Stanford University educational models. The change was not expecting a historical review of the typology or to create a milestone in the evolution of office buildings. It involved a quiet revolution of work organization, making it less hierarchical and more laid-back, albeit with limited impact on the architectural envelope of the buildings.

Clive Wilkinson has recognized that globalized working with business connections across all time zones requires employees to stay longer in their workplace. 'We have clients who have to go to the office at 7 a.m. in the morning in order to connect with London, but then also need to be in the office at 10 p.m. at night in order to connect with India. As a result, there are longer hours and you need to do something with that time.'[8] The reward for staff for their hard work is not a higher salary but the offer of constant fun, blurring the lines between business and leisure. Basketball courts, pool tables, ping-pong tables, slides and computer apps bring play to work and deliberately remove any references to the alienation of mass production. The company provides services and a pleasant working atmosphere. A one-off investment is made in the physical office environment and this investment is recovered when the company negotiates terms and conditions with its employees.

7. Adam L. Penenberg. *Play at Work. How games inspire breakthrough thinking.* Piatkus, 2013.
8. Clive Wilkinson. Designing spaces for new ways of working. *Designboom.* May 2014. http://www.designboom.com/design/clive-wilkinson-on-designing-spaces-for-new-ways-of-working-03-17-2014/

THE OFFICE ON THE GRASS

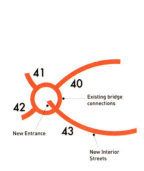

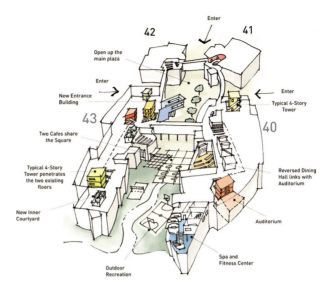

Graduation from Hot to Cold in thirteen workspaces. To the right, sketches of the four buildings juxtaposed. View from the East. Googleplex en Mountain View, Ca., 2005. Clive Wilkinson Architects.

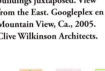

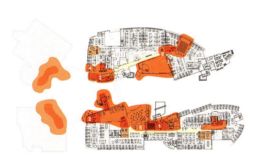

First floor plan

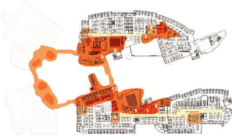

Second floor plan

1 CLUBHOUSE
ACTIVE NOMADIC WORK
OPPORTUNITY FOR CHANCE
ENCOUNTERS

2 BAKERY/COFFEE SHOP
ACTIVE NOMADIC WORK
OPPORTUNITY FOR CHANCE
ENCOUNTERS AND COLLABORATION

3 SUPPER CLUB
ALTERNATIVE DINING SETTING FOR
FOCUSED COLLABORATIVE WORK

4 CONFERENCE
FOCUSED SPACE FOR LARGER
COLLABORATIVE GROUPS

WHITE BOARDS
PROJECTION CAPABILITES

5 LIBRARY
QUIET NOMADIC WORK
VISITOR WORKSPACE

6 I-BAR
ACTIVE NOMADIC WORK
VISITOR WORKSPACE

7 TERRACE
QUIET ALTERNATIVE FOR
NOMADIC WORK
VISITOR WORKSPACE

8 OPEN MEETING
QUIET NOMADIC WORK
VISITOR WORKSPACE
IMPROMPTU TEAM COLLABORATION

9 OPEN HUDDLE
IMPROMPTU TEAM COLLABORATION

10 CLOSED MEETING
FOCUSED SPACE FOR
COLLABORATION
WHITE BOARDS
PROJECTION CAPABILITIES
OPTIONAL AS WAR ROOM

11 HUDDLE ROOM
QUIET NOMADIC WORK

FOCUSED COLLABORATION SPACE
WHITE BOARDS

12 WORKSTATION
QUIET RESIDENT WORK
FURNITURE RECONFIGURABLE
TO MEET TEAM'S NEEDS

13 WORKROOM
QUIET RESIDENT WORK
FURNITURE RECONFIGURABLE
TO MEET TEAM'S NEEDS
PANELIZED FRAMING SYSTEMS
TO ACCOMMODATE JOINING OFFICES
FOR BIGGER TEAMS

THE LIQUID NATURE OF WORKSPACE

Above, collaborative work area, bar counter with surfboards in the public space of the warehouse. On the right, overlapping individual offices on three levels. TBWA/Chiat/Day. Los Ángeles, 1998. Clive Wilkinson Architects.

The starring role in the programme for the fun office is the coffee bar where the brand character comes to the fore. It is the main place for socializing in the company. This is not the canteen of the pre-Modern social condensers which had one specific mission –simply to eat– and which was only for company staff whereas here it has become a new space for non-stop utilization creating dependence, a place to connect, to see and to be seen.

Above and below, facilities at Googleplex in Mountain View, Ca., 2005.
Clive Wilkinson Architects.

THE CONNECTED OFFICE

Millennials were not raised in libraries but in cafés and in connected third spaces. Their work culture comes from college campuses and the essentials are a laptop, a pair of headphones and caffeine.[9] The laptop removes any dependence on a fixed workplace and enables you to permanently move around as much data and entertainment media as you want. The headphones block out the world and create a personalized floating atmosphere which accompanies employees wherever they go while coffee feeds the non-stop activity now free of any dependence on the solar cycle. This is how we might define the mobile connected office.

The Dalles Google Data Center spreads over two industrial 94,000 square-foot buildings staffed by only 80 people due to the high degree of automation. It is located on the banks of the Columbia River, Oregon. It stores e-mails, photos, videos and digital files to be circulated over the Internet and can be accessed by any connected device anywhere on the planet. The same goes for the data centres of the Chinese online giant Alibaba in Hangzhou, Qingdao and Beijing. The interior of the former Western Union building[10] at 60 Hudson Street, NYC is one of the most important Internet nodes in the world where local, national and global fibre optic networks converge. It is the headquarters of Internet content companies guaranteeing greater security and faster data transfer. These data centres located all over the world absorb the physical information contained in the old filing cabinets, convert it to bits, and save it to groups of servers, with minimum staff.

If the generational shift has changed behaviour, it is technology which has altered the way of accessing and storing information. In the workplaces of the creative class and in those dedicated to administrative tasks the unequivocal relationship between the employees and the physical location where the data was kept has been eradicated. The workplace has gained in mobility at the cost of being constantly fed by a supply company. At present, it is the large telecommunications and software firms who pull the strings and set the pace of the evolution of the connected office.

Luchetti and Stone published Your Office is Where You Are[11] over thirty years ago at a time when the Internet protocols had not yet been developed. They announced a profound physical shift, based on mobility, which has become a reality. Nonetheless, the underlying transformation which has occurred in terms of the organization of work and its control strategies has been even more far-reaching.

9. Frank Duffy. *Work and the City*. Black Dog Architecture, 2008.
10. Andrew Tarantola. Gizmodo. 2011. http://gizmodo.com/5858571/one-of-the-most-important-internet-hubs-in-the-world-is-in-manhattan
11. Philip J. Stone, Robert Luchetti. "Your office is where you are". *Harvard Business Review* 63/2, 1985 p. 102-117.

In the 1980s, productivity was the target to be achieved within a given space and time. Today, the path to achieving productivity is by conquering the complicity of employees outside this time and space. If a company is able to get an employee to answer an e-mail when they are dining out with friends, to read a sales department report while travelling on the underground, to take a conference call with a client six time zones away at home, to continue a business meeting in the nearest café... there is no productivity target that cannot be met.

Flexible hierarchies, the opportunity to eat at the workplace, undefined hours and the anywhere culture facilitated by mobile technology have dissolved the solidity of the traditional office. Cafés, hotels, homes, stations and airports... are pervaded with the function of work.

The lobby-bar of the Ace Hotel London Shoreditch, designed in 2013 by Universal Design Studio, interacts with the local area. It is on the ground floor of the hotel where the local community can work. It is a space with climate control, free WIFI and a range of services available to the public: an art gallery, a natural juice bar, toilets and a shared working space.

Workspace in the lobby of the ACE Hotel. Shoreditch, London, 2013. Universal Design Studio.

THE LIQUID NATURE OF WORKSPACE

Filing cabinet in the office of
Frederick Law Olmsted.
at Brookline, Boston, Ma.

THE OFFICE ON THE GRASS

The Dalles Data Center was built on the bank of the Columbia River in Oregon due to low land prices and the tax breaks offered by this State. In the empty areas of the Server Room, motion sensors automatically shut off the lights to save energy. The result is the brightness of the world's data filtered through multicolor LED lights.

THE LIQUID NATURE OF WORKSPACE

1984. Still from the film based upon George Orwell's novel of the same name.

Market Street. Celebration, Fl.

Main Street. TBWA/Chiat/Day. Los Ángeles, 1998. Clive Wilkinson Architects.

12. According to the 2010 census, the number of inhabitants of Celebration is 7,427. http://www.celebrationinfo.com/demo.htm
13. Nicolai Ouroussoff. "A work through the looking glass". *Los Angeles Times*. January 31, 1999. http://articles.latimes.com/1999/jan/31/entertainment/ca-3282
14. Ibid. 13

THE HYPERREAL OFFICE

The concept of hyperreality, formulated in the 1980s, served to clarify phenomena such as Disneyland or Las Vegas and today helps us to understand certain workplaces. Companies wanting to be innovative, in a struggle to keep on talented staff, offer solutions with a visual impact, replacing office cubicles with simulated worlds, rather than incentive payments. The new generation, who have welcomed the virtual décor of the entertainment industry into their lives, prefer a pleasant suggestive environment, far removed from harsh reality, to higher remuneration.

In the experimental microcosm that is Los Angeles, the Celebration Company was launched, a firm promoting the artificial city of the same name promoted by The Walt Disney Company. In reality, Celebration is not even a city but a census-designated place.[12] Its main streets (Market Street and Front Street) are elements reclaimed by New Urbanism to add life to this artificial scheme created from scratch. Indeed Clive Wilkinson Architects, CWA, took the idea for a Main Street-style central axis[13] from Celebration and applied it to the offices of the advertising agency TBWA/Chiat/Day, Los Angeles in 1998.

This project for an ad agency which creates business ploys has become a paradigm shift. It symbolizes escapism in contemporary business environments through a simulated hyperreal space. 'But the Chiat/Day building is also an idealized model of social engineering. Both Utopian commune and Orwellian nightmare, it is a shrewdly designed 'social condensor' whose inhabitants are carefully sealed off from the outside world with their common goal – which is to create profit for their company– the subtle manipulation of public desire.'[14]

Google exported this trend to Europe in 2007. In the headquarters close to downtown Zurich, spaces have been included which would have been unthinkable in an office 10 years ago. A rest area with aquariums, a library with fake books, vinyl flooring with a printed sand pattern, old wooden cable car cabins with checked curtains and artificial snow on the floor, stuffed crocodiles... These are theme park sets which offer exciting fictitious worlds because the real versions are out of reach. The aim is for that spark to catch, to achieve synergy between employees and to light up the fire of inspiration in order to boost corporate creativity levels. This is exquisite alienation.

THE OFFICE ON THE GRASS

Google Hub. Zurich, 2007. Camenzind Evolution.

Coworking Utopic_us. Madrid, 2016. Izaskun Chinchilla.

One of the terraces at coworking space Betahaus Barcelona.

Peter Pan designed by Disney after the character created by James Matthew Barrie in 1904.

THE ADOLESCENT OFFICE

Sam Jacob proclaimed in 2013 the end of the tyranny of the fun office which he defined as 'places of perpetual adolescence, whose playground references sentence their employees to a never-ending Peter Pan infantilism.'[15]

The analytical psychology of Carl Jung established the foundations for one of the most identifiable archetypes of the human psyche: the *puer aeternus*, the eternal child, which has been exploited from the very beginnings of commercial advertising as a sales strategy.[16] The child, as an invincible being, able to overcome all challenges, as a metaphor for the good savage, represents the triumph of the unconscious mind and rebellion against the rationality of modern thought.

Over four generations, from the Silent Generation (those born before 1940) to the Millennium Generation (1981-1995), sociologists have observed a constant mutation towards greater infantilization. Tobias van Schneider left school at fifteen to work in a computer store. He worked as creative director at Spotify for side projects. He states that these projects are only given the go-ahead if they are simple, if it doesn't matter if they fail and if they aren't taken too seriously. This is an attitude that might seem highly irresponsible in a traditional company. However, it illustrates the approach of the creative technology industry which, as it hires young people who have reached adulthood at the turn of the century, aims to remove all remnants of their parents' generation from the office.

15. Sam Jacob. 'Offices designed as fun palaces are fundamentally sinister'. *Dezeen* magazine. 28 February 2013. http://www.dezeen.com/2013/02/28/opinion-sam-jacob-fun-office-design-sinister/
16. Carl Jung. *The psychology of the child archetype. The special phenomenology of the child archetype. The invincibility of the child.* Princeton University Press, 1968 p. 170-173.

THE OFFICE ON THE GRASS

Slide out through the mirror. Kenjiro Sano office. Tokyo, 2010. Schemata Architects.

In the office designed by Schemata Architects and built in 2010 for the graphic designer Kenjiro Sano in Tokyo, the two archetypes of infancy are brought together: Peter Pan and Alice. The passage from the real to the unreal world is made down a tube slide through a looking-glass. The play on scale using oversize lamps shrinks the office users and turns them back into children. It is the transgression of a space with no partitions, which allows employees to focus and brings acoustic comfort at certain points due to the effect created by large semi-circular lamps hanging from the ceiling.

Drawing from *Alice's Adventures in Wonderland*. Lewis Carroll, 1865.

OFFICE SWEET OFFICE

For decades, office work combined with working from home to maintain a good work/life balance, with the resulting reduction of downtime spent commuting to the workplace. Nowadays, there is a bivalent relationship between work and the home. The concept of home working remains but home comforts are also being brought into the workplace. This is a strategy which distorts employee perception —in that the office resembles the home— to make them feel at ease. Furthermore, it is not just about feeling at home but also about colleagues becoming family. For those having recently entered the workforce, the Millennium Generation, it is becoming increasingly difficult to find a job with a long-term contract and as a result, to have the opportunity to get on the ladder to forming a conventional family. Most of their work/leisure time is split between the successive functional spaces, loaded with sensory and emotional experiences.

The actual spatial shell is increasingly less important than the atmosphere provided, than its capacity to build hyperrealities and to bolster personal relationships. The realm of work is dissolved into a heteropia 'capable of juxtaposing in a single real place several spaces, several sites that are in themselves incompatible.'[17]

It has been argued that the atypical friendly relationships encouraged in some companies, also similar to that existing in some coworking centres where your boss or workmate is also your friend,[18] is just another way of silencing employee demands. This is one of the cunning ploys persisting in business. Betahaus centres are more than just coworking centres: 'it's a happy family living in an amazing house'[19] where you can also work. There are communities in Berlin, Hamburg, Sofia, Copenhagen (Republikken), Vienna and also another in the Gràcia area of Barcelona. The latter is a six-storey 21,500 square-foot building with five terraces. There are sub-spaces where according to those in charge: 'We know that sometimes you want to hold some private callings with your mum or your lover. We created this 'Skype Room' so you can have a cosy and secret call with your clients.'[20]

Each applicant has to have a personal interview with a Betahaus member to be accepted into the family as it is necessary to control the atmosphere, to create good vibrations. It is a place to work, learn, and build prototypes but also where you can eat, drink coffee, meet people, enjoy yourself, have parties and you even have a siesta. It is the new workplace with diluted functions built ad hoc for the Millennium Generation.

---

17. Michel Foucault. "Of Other Spaces, Heterotopias." Architecture, Mouvement, Continuité 5 (1984): 46-49.
18. Andrew Maynard quoting Salvoj Zizek. Work/life/work balance. archiparlour: women, equity, architecture. 2012. http://archiparlour.org/worklifework-balance/
19. http://www.betahaus.es/community/
20. http://www.betahaus.es/portfolio/skype-rooms/

THE OFFICE ON THE GRASS

Above, relaxation area in Google Central Headquarters. London, 2012. Penson
Bottom, Coworking space Betahaus Barcelona.

INTERIORS WITHIN INTERIORS

The construction of interiors within interiors has been the resource traditionally used when aiming for focus and privacy in the workplace while also maximising the use of the available space. Flexibility, a prerequisite for modifying the layout of an office, led furniture designers to design compartments independent of the building envelope and this led to the rise of the cubicle. Robert Propst,[21] graphic designer and inventor, who rose to become President of the Herman Miller Research division, created the cubicle. In the 1960s, the Herman Miller company launched an office programme, named Action Office, based on reducing and establishing the working space for each member of staff. In the following decade, this modular element, allowing views over its three panels, was the defining element for building interiors within other interiors.

Clive Wilkinson believes that the first two stages in the modern office which still remain today –the open plan and the cubicle– should be consigned to oblivion. For him, 'cubicles are the worst –like chicken farming. They are humiliating, disenfranchising and isolating. So many American corporations still have them. I'd say 75-80 percent of America is cubicle land. They still want six-feet-high panels around cubicles and I fight clients on this subject constantly because it is so stupid.'[22]

Within the interior of the space his company designed for the Barbarian Group, an Internet advertising firm, in 2014 he installed a huge wavy 1,100-foot object which occupies a large part of the office and references the Fiat test track in Turin.[23] It is a large landscape-table for 125 employees installed in the free space of a standard office building. This orographical item defines its own interiority and creates new relationships concerning the concepts inside/outside and the general space of the office. It has borrowed the idea from other disciplines and applied it to a specific workplace: 'It's about open structure, about making villages in buildings, for taking urban design thinking into large workplaces.'[24] Ever since 1987 when Niels Torp incorporated an interior street with trees into his project for SAS in Stockholm and eleven years later when Clive Wilkinson Architects built the City Advert for the TBWA/Chiat/Day agency, the distinction between interior/exterior has become blurred with public space breaking into the office.

The design of interiors within interiors has become more inventive following the use of references from other disciplines. In 2010 group8 architects chose a nine-metre high former industrial unit

21. Robert Propst. Designers. Products. Herman Miller. http://www.hermanmiller.com/designers/propst.html
22. Claire Thomas. 'Google was cubicle land when we started designing offices for them'. *Dezeen magazine*. March 2014. http://www.dezeen.com/2014/03/17/office-design-google-clive-wilkinson-interview/
23. Elaine Louie. 'Table Manners at Work'. Home&Garden. *The New York Times*. February 2014. http://www.nytimes.com/2014/02/13/garden/table-manners-at-work.html?_r=1
24. Ibid. 22.

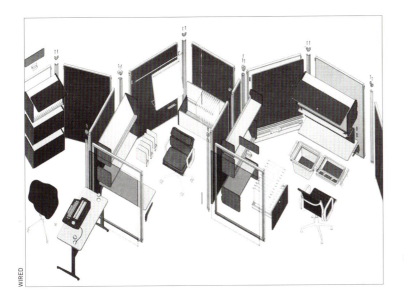

Action Office furniture System designed by Robert Propst in 1968 for the company Herman Miller.

Cluster of containers in group8 offices in Geneva. Switzerland. 2010.

near Geneva as their new HQ. In the interior they installed sixteen cargo containers reclaimed from shipping firms, which they preserved in their original state of decay. Within the envelope of the unit, dichotomy has been created between the large space for socializing –open, abstract, white with natural light from above– and the steel containers which concentrate specific activities such as meeting, relaxing, restrooms... This is the analogy of the village with buildings inside a public space or of one interior inside another.

THE DIVERSE OFFICE

The contemporary workplace has derived from successive compression/decompression. First there was the hierarchical Taylorist office, lacking in sufficient hygiene requirements and with strict hours, which absorbed the private life of the worker. Then came the rational well-lit well-organized office with individual cubicles which allocated each employee the exact amount of air they needed to breathe. Later there was a return to the open landscape office, with free layouts, shrouded in vegetation, which was the forerunner of the de-materialization of the workplace.

Today we are in a far more fluid state which envisages the specialization of space and brand expression. Diversity and identity. The workplace should encompass, not only the two basic tasks already known –individual and group work– but also tasks involving learning and socializing. On the other hand, the brand has come to form part of the programme and its core values should be omnipresent throughout the space.

In a survey conducted by HOK in 2011 using Facebook[25] there were two main responses to the question: What are the current challenges to your productivity when you are at work? These were background noise and the lack of privacy in open-plan offices as well as the usual complaints about heat/cold.

In 2013, Herman Miller launched the Living Office series integrated within the Public Office Landscape, with a wide range of custom design solutions incorporating urban and geographical references: haven, hive, jump space, clubhouse, cove, meeting space, landing, workshop, forum, plaza are the references for the workplaces which aim to embrace formerly non-existent activities such as: chat, converse, co-create, divide&conquer, huddle, show&tell, warm up-cool down, process&respond, contemplate and create.[26]

Adapting these new landscapes to real-time business requirements is a profitable venture for a company. Recently, technology[27] has emerged to manage the use of physical space. This software detects human presence in the workplace allocating vacant workstations to the employees who really need them at a specific time. This can be applied both to workstations shared by several employees and to meeting rooms. This way, space requirements are assessed, taking into consideration that payments on real estate leases are one of the highest corporate overheads. It is a space controller which allocates the workstations according to an algorithm contained in specific software whereby forecasts can be

25. Leigh Stringer. World's largest workplace survey. Using Facebook to transform the workplace. HOK. 2012. http://www.hok.com/uploads/2012/09/17/hokworkplacewhitepapersfinal3.pdf
26. Living Office. Solutions. Products. Herman Miller. 2013. Designed by Yves Béhar/fuseproject. http://www.hermanmiller.com/content/hermanmiller/northamerica/en_us/home/products/solutions/living-office.html
27. AgilQuest's Commander BI technology. http://agilquest.com/

Facebook headquartes at Hacker Way. Menlo Park, Ca.

made for up to ten years from now. Reducing space per employee to 100 square feet may lead to cost savings of between 10 and 20% in the building lease.[28] If the contractual terms are favourable it is also possible to sub-let the resulting vacant space leading to an extra revenue stream. Teleworking and transferring employees to shared collaborative working areas can also save a great deal of money for a company.

The shift between space dedicated to individual work and group work, between focus and collaboration space is also bringing major changes. Forecasts are seemingly contradictory depending on the financial interests of those conducting the evaluation. On the one hand, it is estimated that in twenty years' time the relationship between private space/shared space in an office will shift from 70/30 to 30/70.[29] In 2013, CoreNet, a global association which defends the

28. Martha C. 'White. Start-up chic goes corporate, as couches replace desks'. Commercial. The New York Times. 2013. http://www.nytimes.com/2013/10/09/realestate/commercial/start-up-chic-goes-corporate-as-couches-replace-desks.html?_r=2&

29. Herman Miller. fuseproject. http://www.fuseproject.com/work/herman_miller/public/?focus=overview

interests of corporate offices, released the findings of a survey in which nearly two-thirds of companies questioned stated that the average amount of space per office worker was 150 square feet and just over half projected a future average of only 100 square feet.[30] The space for concentration has been gradually reduced in favour of shared space but everything points to the onset of a 'collaborative space bubble'[31] and it appears that excessive trust has been placed in the abilities of employees to focus in the open-plan office. At Gensler they feel the same: 'despite many workplaces designed expressly to support collaboration, time spent collaborating has decreased by 20%, while time spent focusing has increased by 13%.'[32]

Liquids will leak out of any holes in the container and the transfer between focus and collaboration is increasingly common. The global economy and the configuration of the workplace are closely related.[33] If the economy becomes more participatory and more interdependent the same occurs with the workplace. The only singularity is that the same conditions cannot be applied to all workplaces. Each sector has specific requirements such that there will be companies whose employees can assume greater mobility and others who will want to have permanent control of their workforce which will put constraints on the design of the office.

The most recognizable and most widespread phenomenon is the introduction of a wide range of variations in an aim to have spaces where individuals feel at ease. Less defined areas, without a precise physical border, which spread out and instil an aura of lightness, mobility and inconsistency, are being added on to the individual offices, open-plan offices, meeting rooms and service areas which already existed in the solid modernity.

Compared to the solidity of modern utopia, the contemporary office stands on unstable shifting foundations. According to Zygmunt Bauman, the lack of job security is the natural state of modern liquidity where rates of unemployment have become structural. Workplaces aim to simulate unattainable paradises because: 'in the absence of long-term security, 'instant gratification' looks enticingly like a reasonable strategy.'[34]

30. CoreNet: Office space per workers shrinks to 150 sf. Building Design + Construction. 2013. http://www.bdcnetwork.com/corenet-office-space-worker-shrinks-150-sf
31. Richard Kadzis. Vice President, Strategic Communications for CoreNet Global. Ibid. 30.
32. Gensler. 2013 US Workplace Survey. Key Findings. http://www.gensler.com/uploads/documents/2013_US_Workplace_Survey_07_15_2013.pdf
33. Gensler. It's the Economy. Design Forecast, 2013. http://www.gensler.com/uploads/documents/Gensler_Design_Forecast_01_04_2013.pdf
34. Zygmunt Bauman. *The Liquid Modernity*. Polity Press. 2000, p. 189.

Sources of Inspiration

Elements,

Qualities,

Form,

Green Agenda

Texts and drawings by Javier Mozas

> "To design is always to redesign. There is always something that exists first as a given, as an issue, as a problem. Design is a task that follows to make that something more lively, more commercial, more usable, more user's friendly, more acceptable, more sustainable, and so on, depending on the various constraints to which the project has to answer. In other words, there is always something remedial in design."[1] BRUNO LATOUR

TO DESIGN IS ALWAYS TO REDESIGN

Designing involves working with tools and concepts which vary according to the technology and culture of each moment. The crisis of Modernism has deprived the architect of certain seemingly unchanging resources which had come to be taken for granted. Nature, habitat, energy management, mobility and social responsibility have all replaced components from the traditional discipline. These components, some of which date back to the classic era: the column, the arch, and other essential Modern elements: gravity, lightness or materiality remain elements of intellectual resistance, exclusive standard-bearers of meaning.

Workplaces have not escaped this all-pervading trend and have also been affected by this liquefaction process which is dissolving the basic function of work. Offices and their two main, corporative and speculative, principles which correspond respectively to the selective and the generic, have sought different escape routes. The speculative office has clashed with the envelope and the corporative office has evaporated into meaning.

The speculative office type has been reduced to a form stripped bare of all accessories. The compositional elements have discarded the third Vitruvian principle and have come to worship at the altar of data: square metres, construction costs and return on investment.

The typical corporative office employs architecture to reinforce the corporate brand image, to strengthen brand identity or to deny corporate history. Large multinational corporations diversify their external appearance between the global and the local and adopt a green agenda which is not part of their corporate gene set but which openly serves their business goals.

1. Latour, Bruno. Lecture for the "Networks of Design" meeting of the Design History Society Falmouth, Cornwall, United Kingdom. 2008.

In any of these two scenarios: corporative or even speculative, the architect is the necessary interlocutor yet one who feels naked and toolless. One of the architect's ways of reinforcing the intellectual structure of the building is by going back to the actual discipline. The history of architecture becomes a way of getting a grip on the form. Until now and depending on style preferences, the architect has made use of both close and distant figurative resources but in this new scenario with its complex interactions and changing relationships everything has become less clear: "vague concepts, vague functions, vague roles, vague territories, vague add-ons, vague directions."[2] The Typical Plan involving repetition and indeterminacy is already, by its own merits, part of History and is creating an ever-widening gap between the contemporary and the Modern office.

The following examples aim to clarify the vague sea of intentions which give rise to the form of a workplace. One Pancras Square by David Chipperfield, ÖKK Headquarters by Bearth & Deplazes, Eisgasse House by Max Dudler, Lagerstrasse House by Gigon/Guyer, Allianz Headquarters by Wiel Arets and DNB Headquarters by MVRDV have all had material and ethical dimension analyzed, reclaiming references, highlighting elements or pinpointing qualities in that this might help to understand the sources of inspiration used by the architects. This is how the mental space is constructed from which later inspirational workplaces will be created.

Apple, Google and Facebook are also included. The three companies between them employ 27% of the population of Silicon Valley yet they also bring gridlock to Highway 101, the former Camino Real (Royal Road) which used to link the Spanish missions, on a daily basis. On becoming giant corporations they have replaced their former uninspiring production sites, garages and college campuses, and have set themselves the task of redefining the workplace for the coming years. The inspiration behind each project is rooted in the architects' cultural backgrounds. Once the functional requirements have been overcome, the aim is to satisfy the green agenda by incorporating a vast array of design resources.

Norman Foster resorts to the pure forms generated in the 18th Century, Frank Gehry to the ordinary volume of the most banal construction, whereas BIG and Thomas Heatherwick aspire to build an impossible world using the utopias of a crazy fun era.

2. Ishigami, Junya. *Another Scale of Architecture*. Toyota Municipal Museum of Art. 2010. p. 5.

THE LIQUID NATURE OF WORKSPACE

Element: the Column

The Parthenon
Iktinos, Kallicrates, Phidias
Athens, 447-432 b.c.

When mention is made of the archetypal Doric temple, Greek temples are seen as a catalogue, as a relation of samples which end up becoming a way of generating storeys. Vitruvius tackled this theme from an approach based on the general principles of architecture classified into three groupings[1]: order (taxis), category (genera) and symmetry (symetria). The order sets out the geometrical order, the category (grid) and the tripartite (tripartition). The category defines a code for a set of elements which results in the style: Doric, Ionic, Corinthian or Tuscan. The symmetry creates the rhythm of each of the elements and their relationship with the whole.

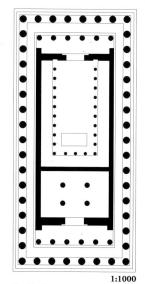

1:1000

The Parthenon.
Peripteral temple.
8 x 17 Doric columns.

1:2000

Two types of ancient Greek temples. Amphiprostyle/pseudoperipteral, on the left and prostyle, on the right.

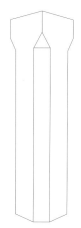 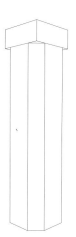 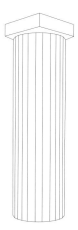

Evolution of Doric Column.

1. Alexandre Tzonis, Liane Lefaivre. *Classical architecture: the poetics of order.* MIT Press. London. 1986. p. 6

Element: the Column

Baloise Park
Valerio Olgiati
Basel, 2014

The column becomes a symbolic element, distanced from classical representation and is moved into the interior of the floor plan as a part of the layout. The column becomes a generating element which is reproduced in three different widths in the facade. The column-house with its gabled roof, as an icon, which also appears in the building floor plan and which is inhabited on the inside, hence becoming a closed space which may house stair shafts in its interior or become a cubicle for more private activities.

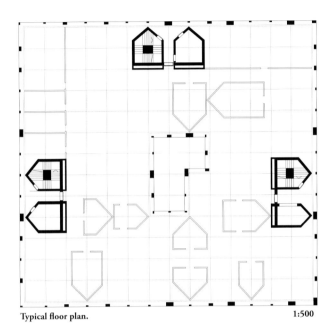

Typical floor plan.   1:500

Facade support element.

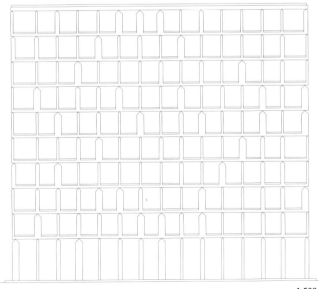

Elevation with the three types of columns.   1:500

THE LIQUID NATURE OF WORKSPACE

Element: the Column

One Pancras Square
David Chipperfield Architects
London, 2008-2013

David Chipperfield was never a Modernist. Throughout his career, he has borne the weight of History on his shoulders and there are conditions such as dematerialization or the lack of thickness of the envelope which he does not feel at home with. During the design process, his hand cries out for thickness and shade lines and this is exactly what glass curtain walls fail to provide. The commission which could sway him the most would be an office building for generic users in the speculative environment of London city centre. It is here where he calls out for intervention from the gods of the past. The classicism of a Greek temple and the 19th Century railway foundry team up to create the temple of work for luxury brands, software companies and headhunting firms.

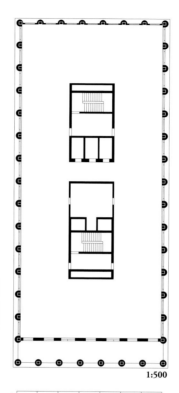

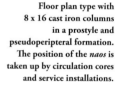
1:500

Floor plan type with 8 x 16 cast iron columns in a prostyle and pseudoperipteral formation. The position of the *naos* is taken up by circulation cores and service installations.

Front elevation with proportions similar to the hotel Il Palazzo by Aldo Rossi in Fukuoka, Japan, where, in a play on composition, the main facade is blind and the pattern is based on amber-coloured Iranian travertine stone columns.

THE LIQUID NATURE OF WORKSPACE

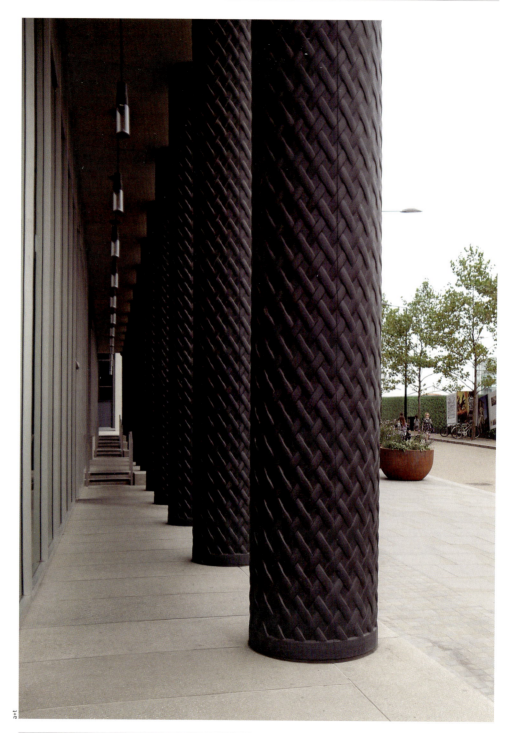

THE OFFICE ON THE GRASS

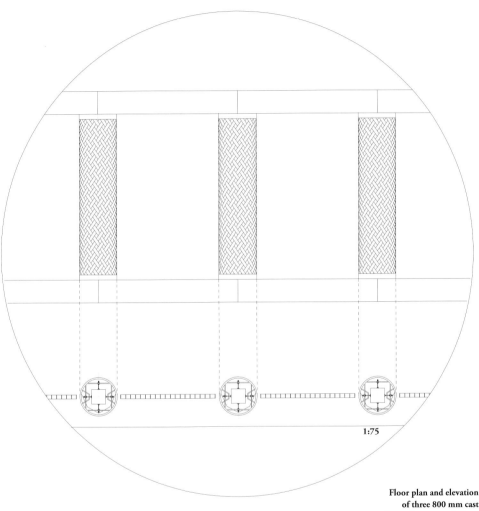

1:75

Floor plan and elevation of three 800 mm cast iron columns, made from salvaged scrap material at the Hargreaves Foundry Halifax. This material reminds us of the Victorian legacy and the site's historical railway links. The motif printed on the outer side of the cylinder refers to the *Bekleidung Theorie* by Gottfried Semper and to the textile origin of the primitive architecture.

THE LIQUID NATURE OF WORKSPACE

Element: the Arch

Al-Azhar Mosque
Author unknown
Cairo, 970-972

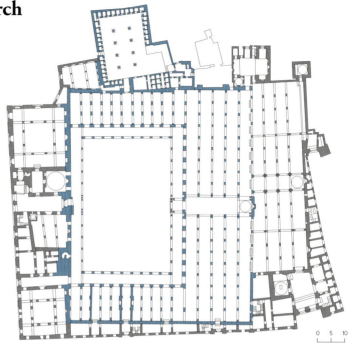

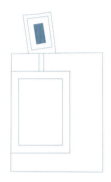

The floor plan is a palimpsest in which the traces of the former construction can be easily recognized, with courtyards, libraries and madrassahs connected by narrow passageways which open out into wider spaces.
The courtyard of columns of the Al-Azhar mosque is a succession of isostatic porticoes with arches on marble columns reinforced with transversal bracing.

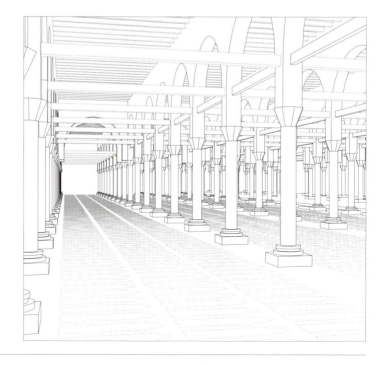

THE OFFICE ON THE GRASS

Element: the Arch

Tama Art University Library
Toyo Ito
Hachioji City (Tokyo), 2007

The Tama public library contains a dual complexity in its structural conception. The lines of the arches are not orthogonal but instead have an interlinked curved hyperstatic layout which stabilizes the construction and is earthquake-proof.

THE LIQUID NATURE OF WORKSPACE

Element: the Arch

Ökk Insurance
Bearth & Deplazes
Landquart, 2012

The appearance of white concrete arches in the centre of a small Swiss town, with little more appeal than the imposing presence of the railway station, must have caused a sensation among inhabitants due to the religious connotations of the courtyards and cloisters. This corporate office for a local insurance company needed to impose its identity and manifest a coherent urban presence. The design for Andrea Deplazes is a process of interaction and synthesis. This is a method which is a feedback loop rather than a linear sequence. In this project, the arch was chosen subjectively and became the core project theme. The strong construction component inherent in the Bearth & Deplazes office is a rethink of the execution of this element by incorporating prefabrication, based on the contemporary demand for repetition and modularity.

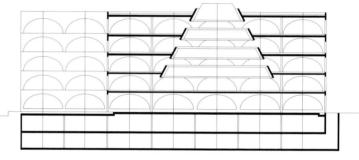

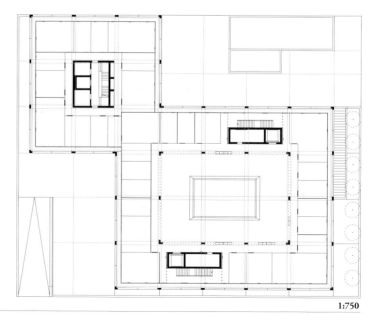

1:750

THE LIQUID NATURE OF WORKSPACE

THE OFFICE ON THE GRASS

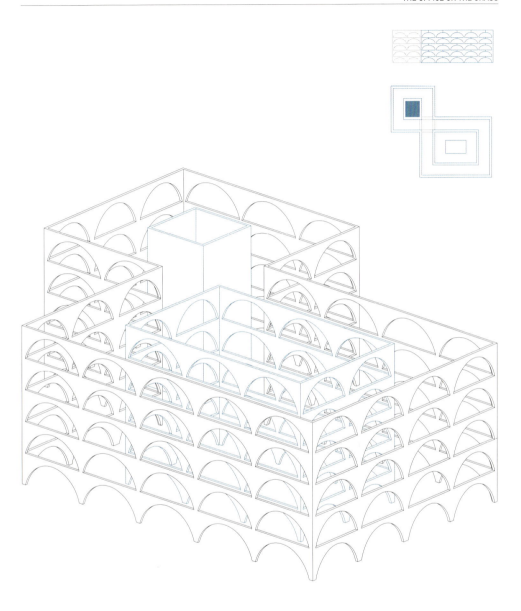

Each one of these two rectangles connected by one vertex seem to be built in succession, as in the case of the Al-Azhar mosque. The largest has a hollow centre whereas the other has a solid core.

Quality: Gravity

Tribune Tower
Ludwig Hilberseimer
Chicago, 1922

Hilberseimer approaches the design of the Chicago Tribune offices as if they were the facilities of an industrial manufacturing unit. "Hilberseimer's [office buildings] are simply the most literal representation of the open-ended logic of capital when it comes to the question of form."[1]

1. Aureli, Pier Vittorio. "The Barest Form in which Architecture Can Exist: Some Notes on Ludwig Hilberseimer's Proposal for the Chicago Tribune Building." *The City as a Project*, 2011.

High-rise Factory
Ludwig Hilberseimer
Chicago, 1922

The open floor plan and the facade, with its uniformly-patterned openings, create their own style, which is associated with financial power and uncompromisingly offers only one representation, that of a stark volume.

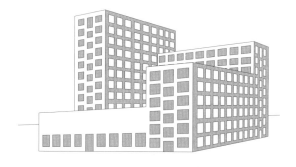

THE OFFICE ON THE GRASS

Quality: Gravity

New Townhall
Vacchini Gmür
Nice, 2000

Power in this case is municipal, with two sturdy volumes which go one step further in their representation of Hilberseimer logic. Dissolving the massiveness into the corners of the building is an allegory of the desire to bring the local authority closer to citizens.

Playing with the missing section of columns on the facade, in a slimming down of the built mass at the edges, is little more than a subtle allegory of how the building dissolves into its setting.

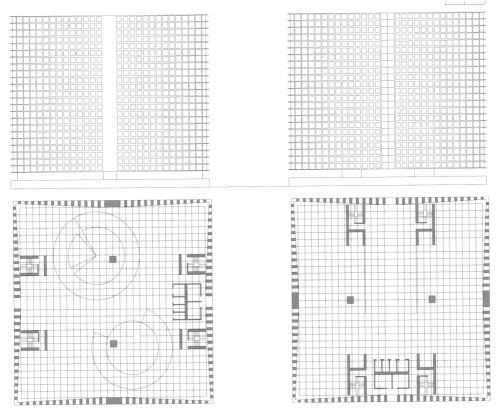

81

THE LIQUID NATURE OF WORKSPACE

Quality: Gravity

Eisgasse House
Max Dudler
Europaallee 21.
Zurich, 2013

In the Eisgasse House by Max Dudler we discover the profound dependence of the creative moment which defined the lines of the Modernist office. What has evolved after ninety-plus years of technological development and new methods of artistic expression? The bare concrete of Hilberseimer has become dark green cast stone, yet the tripartite pattern of the openings, which vary depending on whether they are in the basement, the main body or the crown, take the anchor point of this layout further back in History. The headquarters of the leading Swiss bank was to make no concessions to any styles or fads. The resemblance between this building and the Hilberseimer 1922 factory project indicate that financial power is anchored in the same formal parameters which underpin the current Western economic model.

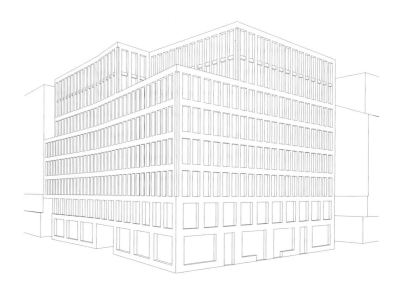

1:500

THE OFFICE ON THE GRASS

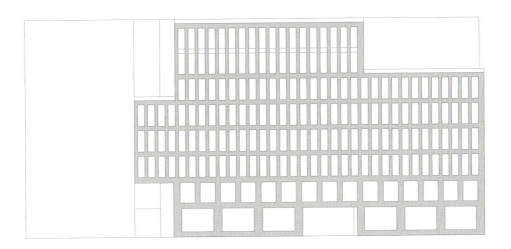

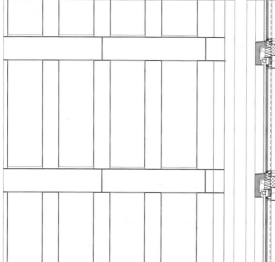
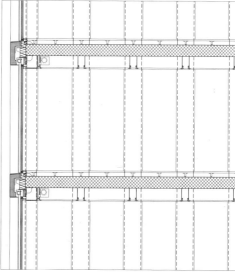
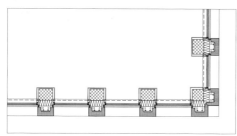

Detail of the facade 1:100

A cladding of massive cast stone sections conceals the window frames, thereby making only two materials visible in the facade: dark green cast stone and glass. Through the addition of local alpine stone of variegated grain (white marble, black basalt, verde Alpi), the dressed stone facade shows a diversity of detail and depth depending on the viewing distance. This gives the impression that the regularly-spaced facade openings have been cut sharply from a monolithic mass, thereby lending the building an imposing *gravitas*.

THE OFFICE ON THE GRASS

Hilberseimer's monolithism is here altered by three deliberate actions: the increased size of the lower openings for commercial reasons, the vertical notches at the indented edges to reduce the massiveness and the setback corner to diminish the perception of the build height.

THE LIQUID NATURE OF WORKSPACE

Quality: Lightness

Skyscraper
Mies van der Rohe
Friedrichstrasse,
Berlin, 1921

The interwar period was a fertile period with the emergence of new working practises and the immediate responses provided by architecture. During this intense creative period an intellectual current emerged which stripped the facade of any structure or decorative element and transformed the envelope into pure reflection.

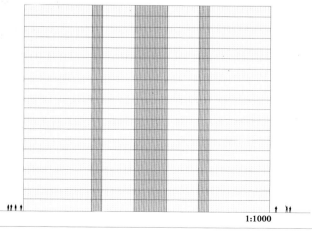

1:1000

Qualities: Lightness

Elbphilharmonie
Herzog & de Meuron
Hamburg,
2003-2017

Contemporaneity adds complexity and hybrid solutions. In the hotel on the upper storeys of the building, the facade curves to incorporate small elliptical openings-vents for the hotel rooms. On the first layer of the Gigon/Guyer building in Zurich (see following project) the ventilation is achieved by simpler means, with small drifts of the glass.

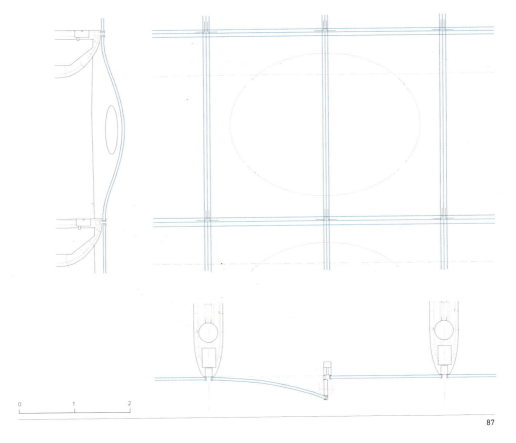

0 1 2

Quality: Lightness

Lagerstrasse House
Gigon/Guyer
Europaallee 21.
Zurich, 2013

Gradation could be determined in office building architecture, from the massive corporeal nature of the concrete building to the dematerialization of the glass prism. This process did not coincide with the temporal sequence of its conceptualization in that although the transition was thought up by the 1920s intellectual avant-garde, its implementation was not accompanied by any technological progress. In the Gigon/Guyer building, Europaallee 21, the Mies glass mutates into a glazed double facade with a fine mesh of golden aluminium on the inside of the first layer. The Hochhaus by Hilberseimer and the Glasshaus by Mies make contact on the south-east corner of the Europaallee 21 and it is here that the leap of perception occurs. The material facade of Dudler comes into contact with the evanescent reflections of Gigon/Guyer.

Materiality and immateriality are mere centimetres away from each other and internal negotiations were required between the three architecture teams involved in the project.

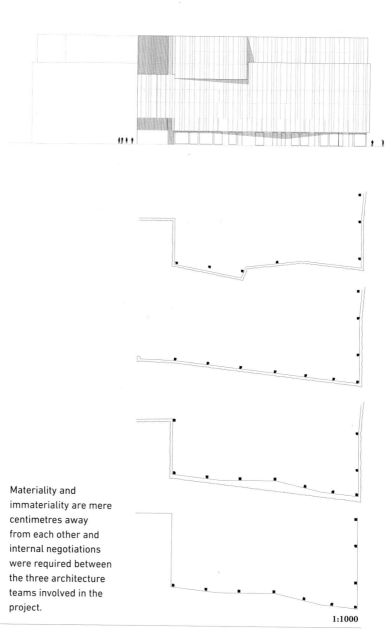

1:1000

THE OFFICE ON THE GRASS

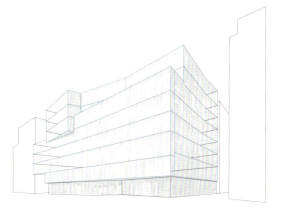

This volume is broken up on each storey and in each element to eschew any associations with Hilberseimer's parallelogram and for it to look more like Mies' faceted prism.

The lightness of the facade does not mean transparency. The glazed panes contain a golden metallic insert which results in the external layer providing sound insulation against street noise, wind protection for the sun blinds and visual screening from the outside, with no detriment to the views from the inside.

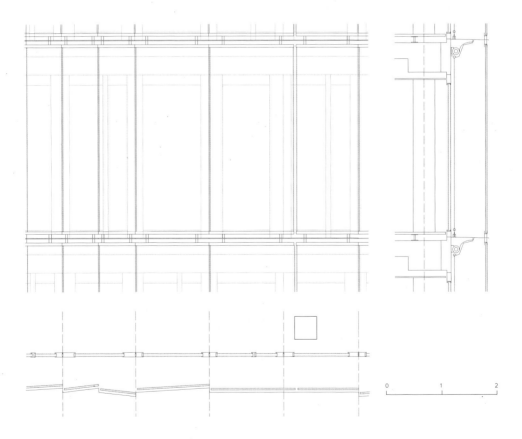

THE OFFICE ON THE GRASS

Joël Tettamanti

THE LIQUID NATURE OF WORKSPACE

Quality: Materiality

The Economist
Alison and Peter Smithson
London, 1959-1964

The travertine of the facade in The Economist is combined with the reinforced concrete to produce an effect of porous plain textures, with a marked relief which lends the buildings designed by the Smithsons the same sensation of verticality as a Greek temple.

Peter Smithson. Photograph of the peristyle of the Temple of Apollo in Bassae, Greece. Included in article "A parallel of the orders" in *Architectural Design*, 1966.

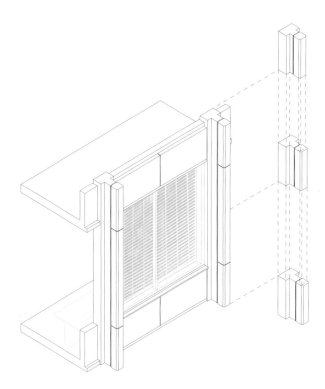

THE OFFICE ON THE GRASS

The corporeal nature of the travertine is manifested in the shade lines of its edges. The underlying reason for the high-rise stepped components is the same as the emphasis on the columns in Greek temples, namely to enhance the aesthetic experience of the trained spectator and to correct the optical image captured by the human eye, by identifying it with its geometric reality.

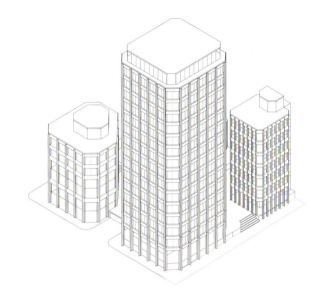

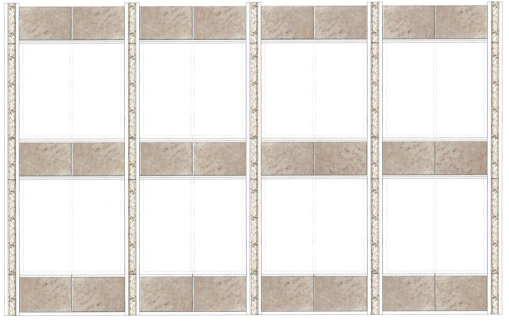

1:100

THE LIQUID NATURE OF WORKSPACE

Qualities: Materiality

Allianz Headquarters
Wiel Arets Architects
Wallisellen, 2014

In the Allianz headquarters in Wallisellen, the materiality of the facade is other-worldly and is a mere impression on the retina. Vittorio Magnago Lapugnani, who drew up the plan for the Richti district of Wallisellen, came up with a structure of closed blocks in the style of 19th Century town planning. Wiel Arets, despite his rigorous respect for alignments, flees from the supposed solidity and organization of openings and turns the materiality of the commission on its head by building a smooth curtain wall resembling an even marble facade.

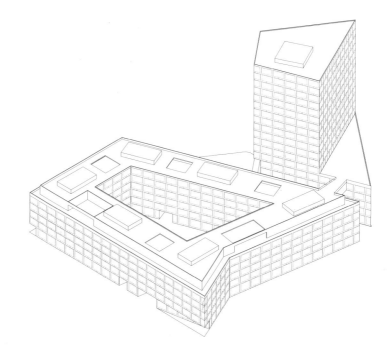

(Left) Barcelona Pavilion, 1929. Image of King Alfonso XIII the day of the official reception. In the original building, the directionality of the marble veining was far less evident.
(Right) The Barcelona pavilion after the 1986 reconstruction. Image of the green marble in the pond with the symmetry of the veins.

THE OFFICE ON THE GRASS

Yet the most striking feature in this facade is not the play on the virtual nature of the stone but rather the construction system used which incorporated independent off-site workshop-built elements. Each module is a dry-air sealed 30 cm thick cavity into which an electronically controlled curtain is inserted. Each component is 2.70 m wide and between 3.70 and 8.00 m high, according to its position on the facade. The design of the envelope is related, from a construction and HVAC perspective, with the false ceiling which works as an interior fifth facade. This comprises 1.35 m sided square aluminium panels, perforated with a traditional Swiss eaves pattern, which enable the air to circulate and also function as noise absorbers.

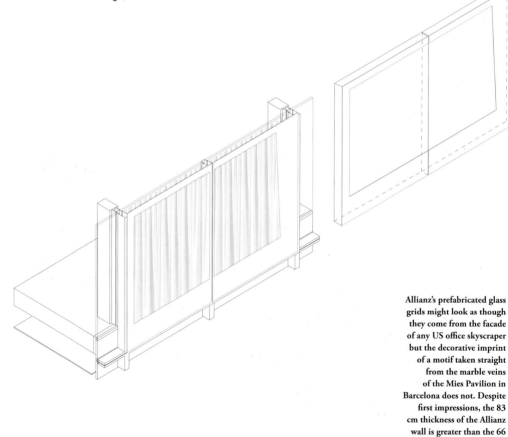

Allianz's prefabricated glass grids might look as though they come from the facade of any US office skyscraper but the decorative imprint of a motif taken straight from the marble veins of the Mies Pavilion in Barcelona does not. Despite first impressions, the 83 cm thickness of the Allianz wall is greater than the 66 cm thickness of the same building in The Economist.

THE OFFICE ON THE GRASS

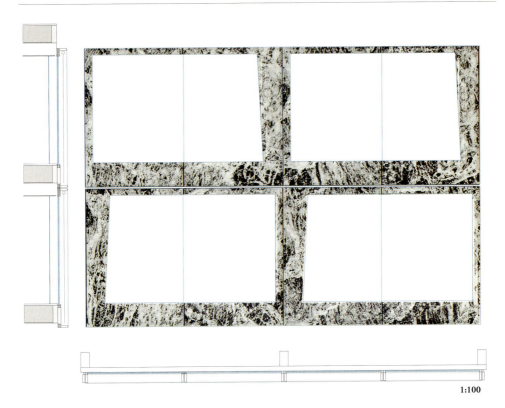

1:100

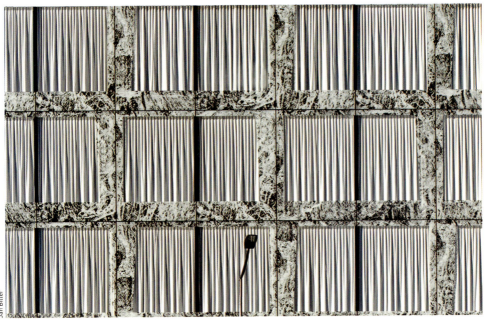

Form: Removing

Giant Hotel
Henri Sauvage
Paris, 1927

The move away from the hierarchical axes of the Beaux-Arts school, via the abstract Modernist mesh, to the support lines of Dutch structuralism has been a complicated path in terms of adapting its programme to the Cartesian grid.
Henri Sauvage invented the stepped building (*immeuble à gradins*) in 1909 as a solution for the health issues present in Paris at the time.
The stepped volume leaves a large void within, which has little use as a living space and is occupied in this case by a large swimming pool, four tennis courts, parking for 500 vehicles, a cinema and a theatre.[1]
Sauvage wanted to repeat this model, as if it were a prefabricated mould, and in 1912 patented a solution which was later used in a number of collective housing buildings.

1. Minnaert, Jean-Baptiste. *The Architectural Drawings of Henri Sauvage*. Routledge 1994. p. 400.

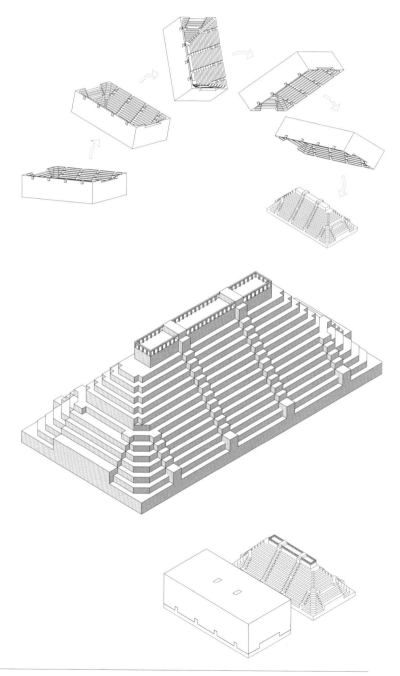

Form: Removing

DNB Headquarters
MVRDV
Oslo, 2012

The contemporary speculative building has made the ideal type suffer further, in this case due to the demands of the market, the interests of developers and the eagerness to prioritize form. Elements, units, cells or modules have become pixels, on or off, depending on whether they are full or empty, and the building layout is no longer dependent on the programme. Sightlines, sunlight, mixed uses, and internal routes have broken with geometrical compactness and ripped open the belly of the building to stark public exposure.

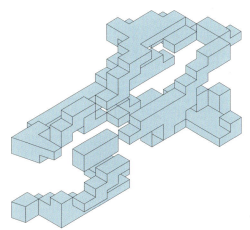

Glazed pixels

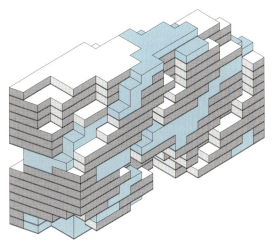

Total volume

THE LIQUID NATURE OF WORKSPACE

THE OFFICE ON THE GRASS

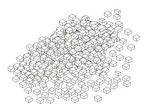

Removed pixels

The Barcode urban plan, designed by MVRDV for the new Bjorvika district, proposes a proximity between volumes which requires the buildings to be sculpted to let in daylight. In the case of the DNB bank headquarters, the strategy involves pixelating the total solid of the spacious 3D form and removing the excess modules. This enables the permitted built volume to be obtained and also provides favourable orientations and views. On the other hand, by extracting the modules a chain-linked route of openings is created which runs around the whole building in all directions. This is both a circulation system and a concatenation of recreation and observation spaces from which users have cross-sightlines of the interior and can enjoy visual relationships.

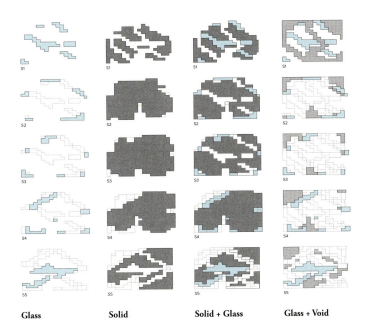

Glass   Solid   Solid + Glass   Glass + Void

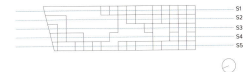

101

Green Agenda: Secluding

Saline Royale
Claude-Nicolas Ledoux
Arc-et-Senans, 1775

Second project fot the Royal Saltworks at Arc-et-Senans.[1] General floor plan according to the Carte Génerale des environs de la Saline de Chaux. The centre of the circle is set aside for the management building. The value of the geometry, the hierarchy of the Masonic architecture and the creation of a parallel world with an initiation route were all taken into consideration by Ledoux as he describes his visit to the saltworks.[2]

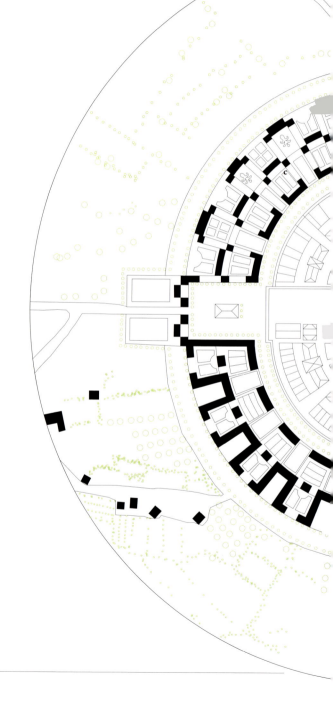

1. Ledoux, Charles-Nicolas. *L'architecture considérée sous le rapport de l'art, des moeurs et de la législation.* Paris, 1804. Plate 14.
2. Vidler, Anthony. *Claude-Nicolas Ledoux.* Birkhäuser, 2006.

THE OFFICE ON THE GRASS

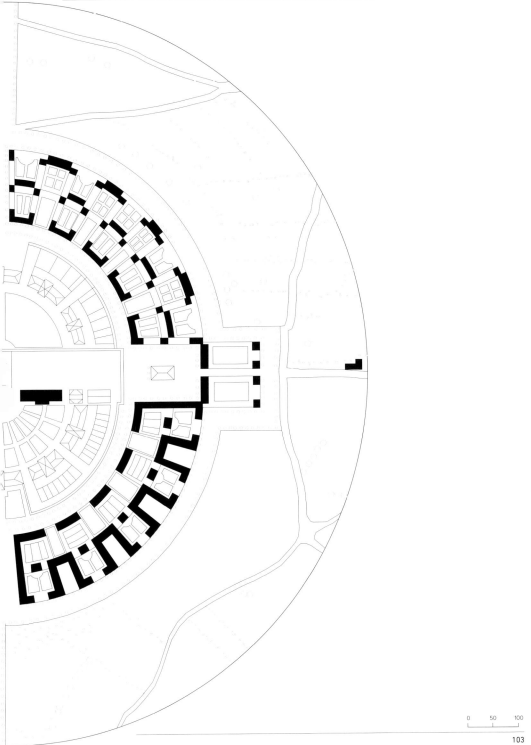

THE LIQUID NATURE OF WORKSPACE

Green Agenda: Secluding

Apple Campus 2
Foster + Partners
Cupertino, Ca.,
2009-2017

The new Cupertino Apple campus is all geometry. Even the address is a reference to the unit and the limit: One Infinite Loop. All is isolation and privacy: bestowed by an insurmountable circular wall and all is nature: a reclaimed green environment. The centre is a void, with no quantity, like the number zero, surrounded by a choir of different types of maple trees. The car park is hidden from sight or buried in a limbo which distances it from the paradise set aside only for the chosen people. Norman Foster said that the circle was not the first choice but that this was the geometric location where the corporate culture of a brand such as Apple merges with the desires and inspiration of the architect.

THE OFFICE ON THE GRASS

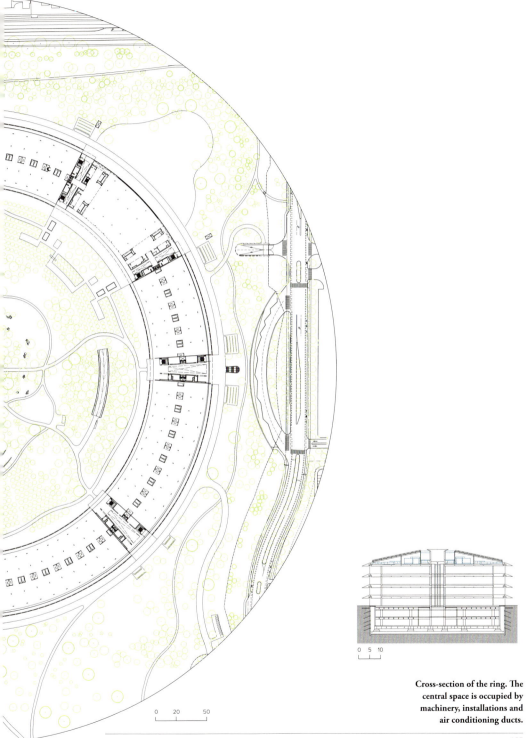

Cross-section of the ring. The central space is occupied by machinery, installations and air conditioning ducts.

Green Agenda: Remediating

Tipi Tents
Sioux Tribe
Dakota, 1862

The lightest tent we know of is the so-called "tee-pee" used traditionally by the Dakota tribe. Their settlements were formed by three or four concentric circles of tents. The central space was set aside for the meeting area of the council or the tents housing the tribal medicines. Over time and due to wear and tear, the skins used to make the tents become increasingly transparent and at night the light from the interior was clearly evident as if they were made from a transparent material.

Sioux settlement in Camp Release during the Dakota War of 1862.

THE OFFICE ON THE GRASS

Green Agenda: Remediating

Drop City
Steve Baer,
Buckminster Fuller
Trinidad, Co.,1965

Drop City was a community founded by artists.
The domes built were based on Steve Baer and Buckminster Fuller models with timber frames and salvaged scrap materials.

United States Pavilion Expo 67
Buckminster Fuller
Montreal,1967

The Montreal Biosphère, the former USA pavilion for the Universal Exposition of 1967 was designed by Buckminster Fuller to house an exhibition programme on seven storeys. It is 76 metres in diameter and 62 metres in height. The form is an icosahedron made up of pentagons inserted inside a hexagonal layout which are then sub-divided into equilateral triangles

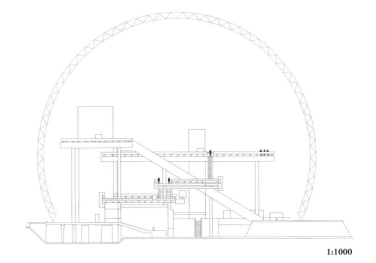

1:1000

107

Green Agenda: Remediating

Google North Bayshore
Big, Heatherwick studio
Mountain View, Ca.,
2015-

The Bjarke Ingels and Thomas Heatherwick generation is not Foster's, nor Gehry's. In 1965, when Drop City was built in southern Colorado or when Buckminster Fuller built the Montreal Biosphère for the Expo 67, they were not yet born. However, the Drop City hippie culture and the controlled climate of the Fuller dome are still cultural milestones which generate unattainable utopias. The fabric material of the Native American teepees was transformed into a double layer of solar glass containing a reinforced membrane which envelops four sites with stacked prefabricated elements. This is the overlap of two worlds: the amorphous world over the regular world, Frei Otto's Olympic roof over Richard J. Diterich's Metastadt system.

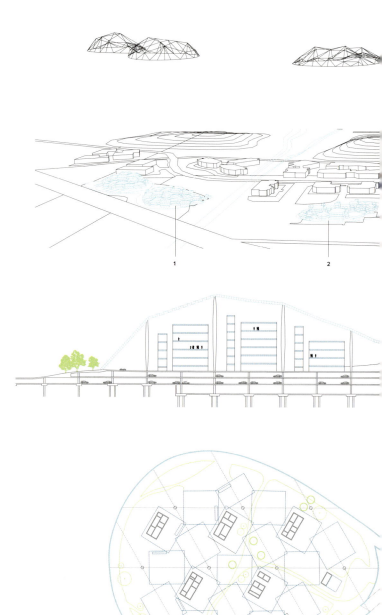

THE OFFICE ON THE GRASS

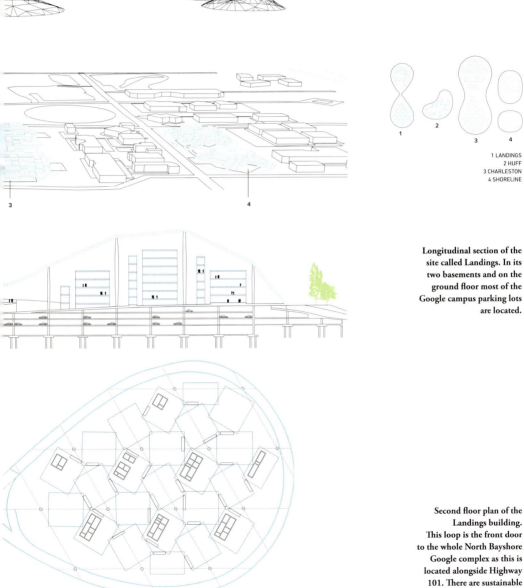

1 LANDINGS
2 HUFF
3 CHARLESTON
4 SHORELINE

Longitudinal section of the site called Landings. In its two basements and on the ground floor most of the Google campus parking lots are located.

Second floor plan of the Landings building. This loop is the front door to the whole North Bayshore Google complex as this is located alongside Highway 101. There are sustainable transport links between this and other sites.

Green Agenda: Camouflaging

Shopping Malls
United States, 1956-

If we identify the architecture of the US shopping malls as the familiar forms referred to by Venturi and Scott Brown, we are given an insight into the origins of MPK 20, the new Facebook campus in Menlo Park. The environmental agenda does the rest and in an act of atonement conceals the parking bays which are visible in other shopping centres. The Albany Walmart Supercenter is the ugly duckling of all the big-box stores, MPK 20 the swan.
The floor plan of the Menlo Park Facebook building differs little from that of a Walmart store. The slight distortion in the orthogonal shape of the smallest boxes forming the whole is the only non-standard feature tolerated by Gehry in the design of the form. The storage spaces for private vehicles are also transformed and, rather than being left exposed, are hidden from sight below the building, as if they were a source of embarrassment.

"Artistically, the use of conventional elements in ordinary architecture -be they dumb door knobs or the familiar forms of existing construction systems- evokes associations from past experience. Such elements may be carefully chosen or thoughtfully adapted from existing vocabularies or standard catalogues rather than uniquely created via original data and artistic intuition."[1]

1. Robert Venturi, Denise Scott Brown. "Ugly and Ordinary. Architecture or the Decorated Shed. Theory of ugly and ordinary and related and contrary concepts". *Forum*. December, 1971. p. 48.

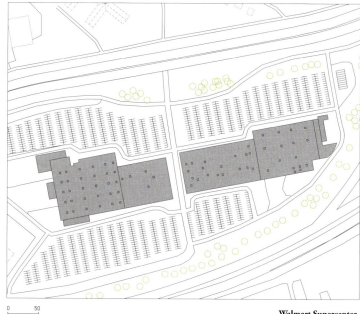

**Walmart Supercenter.
Crossgates Commons 141
Washington Ave Ex. Albany,
NY 12205.**

THE OFFICE ON THE GRASS

Green Agenda: Camouflaging

Facebook
Headquarters MPK 20
Gehry Partners
Menlo Park, Ca.,
2015

Roof and car park floor plan.

THE LIQUID NATURE OF WORKSPACE

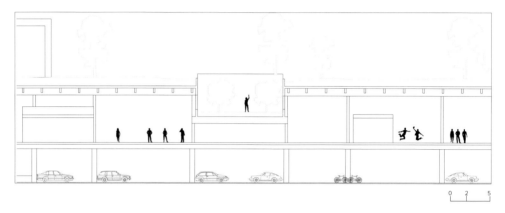

The green roof sinks down and folds over to display the green experience from the interior.

THE OFFICE ON THE GRASS

The new head office, a 280,000 m³ built volume, has been sandwiched between two spaces of atonement: the Garden of Eden on the roof and the Grotto in the parking lot.
In the second decade of the third millennium it would not have been environmentally correct to leave the 1,500 asphalted parking spaces and the roads visible –nosy neighbour Google would only have gone and exposed them to a planetary audience. So the cars are parked on the ground floor but concealed under the office storeys and only the sky blue bicycles, the shuttle linking the two sites and the collective limousine-like white buses which pick up and drop off the employees in the San Francisco bay area can be seen from above. A few cars shyly peek out from under the edges of the concrete slab but no worry the satellites cannot see them.
Seven metres up stand the rooftop trees. Planted in 13,834 m³ of soil, they are already mature and represent the most common native species. The park's 3.6 hectares make it larger than the Grand Trianon in Versailles and maintenance is far more sustainable with drought-resistant grass and shrubbery. There are earth paths and rest areas dotted around with names such as Palo Duro, Timucuan, Duero Valley...
The Facebook roof is more than just a terrace, more than just a garden. It is a reachable Garden of Eden. Facing a horizon of swampland and backing onto a forest of detached houses in Hamilton Avenue, the employees come up here to bond with the landscape without unbonding from their screens. Work goes on in every single corner of this building. Furthermore, the roof is what the satellite will relay to the rest of the world: a large park, instead of the standard service roof; the envy of the neighbours. Who could resist giving it a like?

Above, seating area on the roof garden, with the salt ponds of the San Jose Bay in the background.
Below, the car park hidden under the workspace.

THE INTERIOR

"Mark believes that the office should be a reflection of the company", says a Facebook employee, "it looks like a building site because we are at the start of a project which is only 1% complete". More than a building site, the office resembles a converted industrial unit, with an exposed metal structure of engineering-works dimensions, a flexible plate which functions as a provisional false ceiling and grey carpet-tile flooring separating the work areas from the circulation areas which are polished concrete. As far as the eye can see a cloud of service installations floats above the heads of members of staff, with 80 lanterns hanging from the roof between the air ducts, the cable trays, the lighting, the smoke detectors and the connections which whimsically lead down to each work station. Here the shell strips itself naked.
Unlike the former Facebook headquarters, –just on the other side of the Bayfront Expressway– integrated into a cluster of small Disneylandish buildings where some 5,000 staff still work, the all-in-one model for the new head office has fewer chinks in its armour for escapism. The same ceiling and the same flooring, present in the large canteen, in the break-out areas, in the work areas and in the kitchenettes scattered around the floor plan, remind us that we are here to work, either from a fixed desk or from a fake Shaker chair. The message is all too clear: the world of fantasy which reigned during the early years of corporate growth has been left behind on the other side of the private mirror-tunnel running under the expressway, in the former offices. Now that Mark has come of age, the new Facebook building belongs to the world of adults.

THE OFFICE ON THE GRASS

Changing Roles

JAVIER MOZAS

These pages suggest a game and a conversation between two buildings. Lever House, SOM, New York, 1952 and Shenzhen Stock Exchange, OMA, Shenzhen, 2013. Despite the significant differences in terms of scale (the Shenzhen building is almost three times the size of the New York one) the basic layout could be summed up as a tower and a low body in both cases. In the first case, the horizontal block, which is not perfectly regular, rests on columns and is two-storeys high. In the second case, the cantilevered part is rectangular, includes three storeys and is cut off from the tower by a high-rise void.

Each is a result of the spirit of its time. They both display a boisterous arrogance as if they felt they were being observed, all too aware all too aware of their leading role on the urban stage.

The conversation between them is fleeting yet shows us how they are dissatisfied with both their form and their structural system. For this reason, they decide to swap roles. Lever House raises the horizontal block and positions it to float at mid-rise level and Stock Exchange takes the weight off its cantilever by slipping on a pair of stilettos to support itself on the ground. The result is an International Style, that of Lever House, structurally pushing the boundaries and a Post-modernism, that of Stock Exchange; no irony, no showing off. All this is carried out to display, with this exchange, how they both come from the same creative urge, which is none other than the, more or less, wavy line of modern progress.

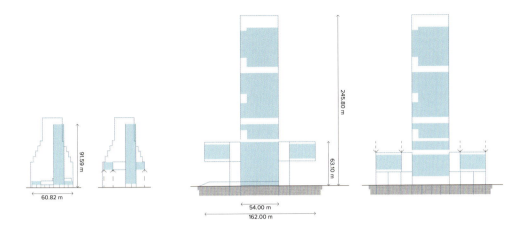

*A Conversation**

Lever House: What's up? How are you doing?
Shenzhen Stock Exchange: Who's calling?
LH: It's me Lever, from Manhattan.
SSE: Ah! Sorry but I was busy trying to explain to my public where they should enter. They don't seem to understand that the Stock Exchange staff have to enter from the east and the clerical staff from the west. That's what Rem told me.
LH: And the garden. How's that going? Me, I'm delighted with Isamu. He designed a low maintenance courtyard full of modern sculptures. I don't know about you.
SSE: Petra came here a few months ago to carry out some finishing touches but the local gardeners got the message. The problem I have is pollution. Some days I can't even breathe.
LH: Yes, that's the problem with us being so metropolitan. But the worst thing for you is those two heavy saddle bags weighing you down every day. Me on the other hand, my podium is well-rested. Although I would like to get more air and get to kick off these heels.
SSE: Good, good! You know you have to instil optimism in the markets and for the stock exchange what goes up is good but if you want, we can do a swap. I'll lend you the idea of the floating podium and I'll try your shoes on.
LH: OK but if I don't like it we'll swap back.
SSE: OK. Let's try.

*This conversation is the continuation of another previous one which took place between Lever House and Seagram Building, included by Wim Eckert in "Park Avenue. Accidental Conversation."
Piet Eckert & Wim Eckert: E2A *Architecture*, Hatje Cantz, 2012.

CHANGING ROLES

This is a dual challenge. Firstly, the challenge to break away from the stepped setback of the 1950s Manhattan buildings and to raise the stock exchange office into the Shenzhen air, showing that the speculative stock market works with shares and equities which are not subject to the laws of gravity. In SSE the high cost of the structural solution was justified by the eagerness to give prominence to form which, due to its differentiation, has managed to bring good financial returns owing to the financial services sector's voracious appetite for exclusivity. If in Lever House unidirectionality is the driving force behind Modernist progress, in SSE there is a constant yin and yang: interior and exterior, public and private, data and art, aesthetics and function, building and garden, curtain wall and exoskeleton, Modernism and Post-Modernism, asymmetry and symmetry, frontal and diagonal, solidity and weightlessness...

Lever House was only allowed to have its tower rise vertically from the base, due to the fact that there was sufficient distance between the building and Park Avenue and that the ground floor was to be converted to a public space with a courtyard with sculptures by Isamu Noguchi. Lever House. Skidmore, Owings and Merrill. New York, 1952.

THE OFFICE ON THE GRASS

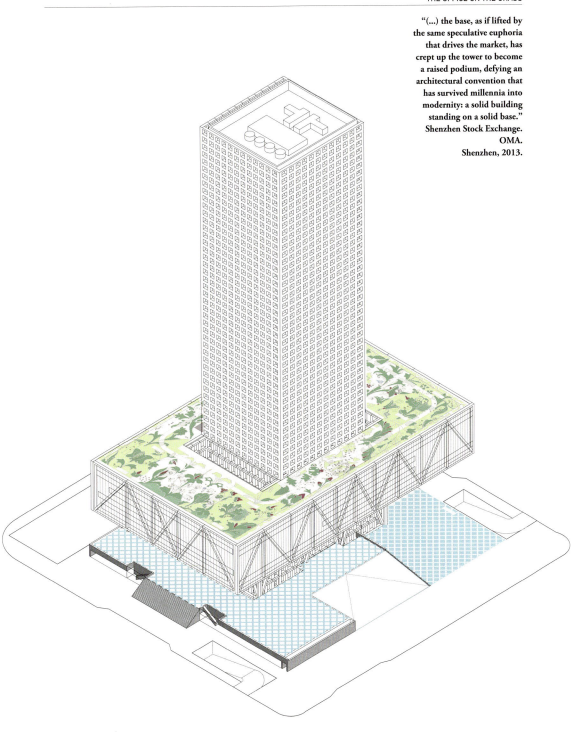

"(...) the base, as if lifted by the same speculative euphoria that drives the market, has crept up the tower to become a raised podium, defying an architectural convention that has survived millennia into modernity: a solid building standing on a solid base."
Shenzhen Stock Exchange.
OMA.
Shenzhen, 2013.

CHANGING ROLES

**Lever House
transformed into
The New Headquarters for the
Shenzhen Stock Exchange.**

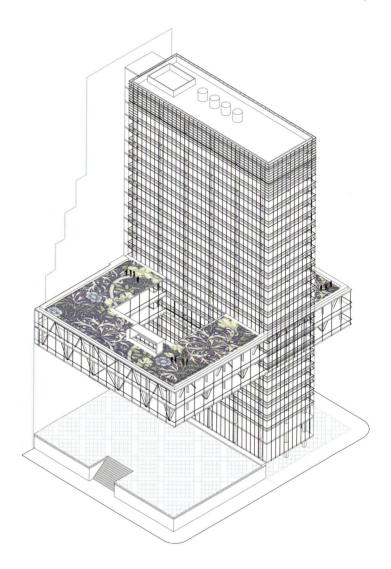

The Lever House Modernist garden has been given a William Morris look, the floating podium has had two storeys added for structural reasons and the ground floor paving has been raised and given a diagonal pattern.

THE OFFICE ON THE GRASS

The New Headquarters for the Shenzhen Stock Exchange transformed into Lever House.

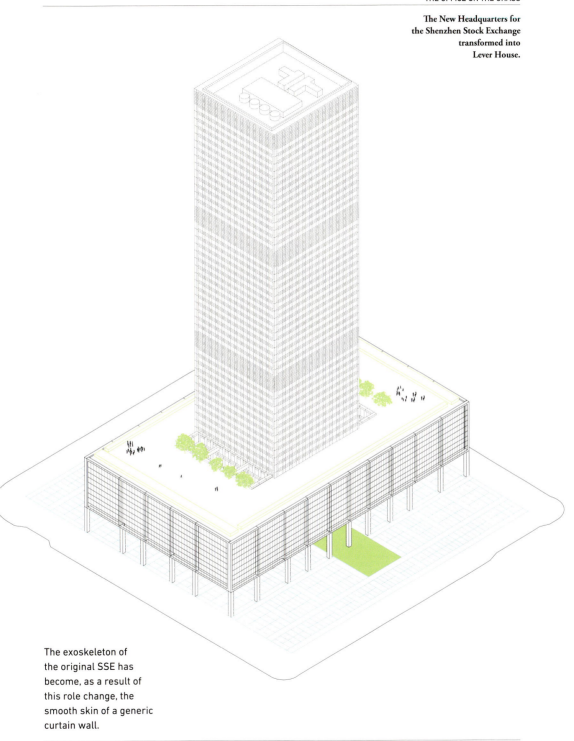

The exoskeleton of the original SSE has become, as a result of this role change, the smooth skin of a generic curtain wall.

Glossary

*Ongoing catalogue of new concepts related
to the work environment.*

Accelerated Serendipity

Higher probability of positive unexpected breakthroughs resulting in collaboration between people with different interests but with the same pro-active approach to life.

Adhocracy

Adhocracy is a term made popular by Alvin Tofler in 1970 and researched by Robert H. Waterman Jr. for his book *Adhocracy: The power to Change*, 1993. This term defines a new type of work organization, with greater decision-making and minimum hierarchy and bureaucracy, capable of adapting to the implementation of specific time-based tasks.

Accelerated Serendipity

Campus Madrid
Madrid, 2015
Jump Studios

The Google HQ Campus Madrid, located in a refurbished factory, aims to establish itself as a world-class hotbed of business creativity. Along with London, Sao Paolo, Tel Aviv and Warsaw this Campus promotes encounters and collaboration between entrepreneurs with different interests. This space can be used to access key resources for the development of new ideas.

Coworking space.

Encounter space.

GLOSSARY

Better Together Mentality

Way of thinking and acting of individuals who meet up to harness energy and knowledge in an aim to reach their target.

Better Together Mentality

Yardhouse
Sugar Island, London,
2014
Assemble

Yardhouse is a model work space for artists promoted, designed, implemented and managed by Assemble. The project, built on a brownfield site close to the architects' office, aimed to build a low-cost prototype which could be replicated on other vacant lots. By cutting down on materials and processes as far as possible, the execution was based on using readily available and transportable generic elements, eschewing sophisticated techniques and processes and facilitating adaptability to different requirements. A timber framework and an enclosure common in industrial units were upgraded with artisan self-construction processes as in the case of the coloured cement panels. Each user can subsequently customize their space.

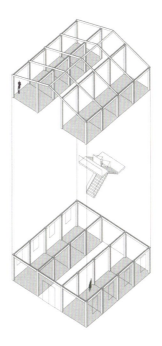

Clan Culture

Coined by Bruce M. Tharp in 2005, this takes place in companies which value cohesion, commitment and staff loyalty to reach productivity targets. Companies practising clan culture are like families and their managers are seen more as paternal advisers than bosses.

Clan Culture

LIN Office Space
Berlin, 2012
LIN Architects

A 4,300 square feet space, where a library used to be, has been converted to an architect's office by demolishing the interior walls and installing raised flooring. The different work spaces have been organized using modular storage shelves. The permeability of the shelving means the visual connection between the areas is maintained. Classifying the entire contents of the office on a spatial basis is a way of analysing those functions which are considered part of the discipline. It also becomes a document referencing the state of the profession in the early 21st Century.

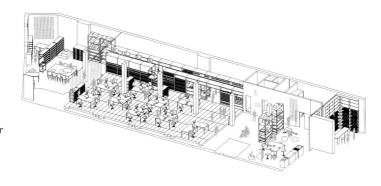

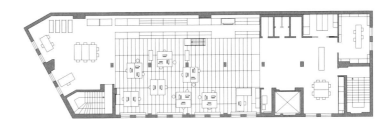

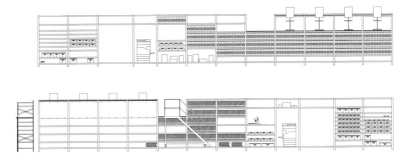

Coworking Space

Working space shared with other independent professionals carrying out different tasks. The term was first used by software developer Brad Neuberg who in 2005 set up the shared space Spiral Muse in San Francisco.

Coworking Space

Club Workspaces
London, 2013
Studio Tilt

By using very simple craft-based technology and low-cost materials, Studio Tilt propose solutions according to the activity and the continuity. The seating stand is the most multifaceted item –it serves as a rest place, for casual meetings, watching events...– the articulated tables provide a larger workspace for specific times and the folding tables are for members who want to have their own area with optional storage space. A curtain divides the space in two when events are on.

Club Chiswick.

Club London Bridge.

1 SKYPE SPACE
2 TOUCHDOWN WORKING
3 DEDICATED WORKING
4 FOCUSED WORKING
5 BREAK OUT
6 COFFEE
7 BANDSTAND
8 EVENTSPACE
9 ENTRANCE
10 COWORKING

1 MEETING
2 DEDICATED WORKING
3 TOUCHDOWN
4 TEAM
5 COWORKING
6 KITCHEN
7 EVENTS AND BREAKOUT

Club Chiswick. Floor plan layout 1:500

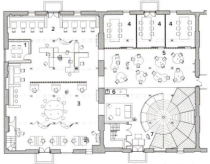

Club London Bridge.

Creative Class

Social group of professionals who have a decisive influence on the post-industrial economy through creation, knowledge and innovation. The term was coined by economist and sociologist Richard Florida in his book *The Rise of the Creative Class*, 2002.

Cubicle Farm

Open-plan office divided into individual semi-closed compartments in which employees are audio-visually isolated. The cubicles are built with panels and modular elements which can be adapted according to corporate requirements. Robert Probst is held to be the inventor of this much-reviled element even though it was merely a cost-driven deviation from his Action Office system, designed for Herman Miller Inc. in 1968.

Creative Class

Hanahaus in Varsity
University Avenue, Palo Alto, Ca.

Besides functioning as a workplace, this cafe is a meeting place for investors and starters, typical of the entrepreneurial ecosystem generated by Stanford University, located only one mile away.

Cubicle Farm

Office Space
USA, 1999
Mike Judge

The film Office Space portrayed the atmosphere of the cubicle farm, where each employee is isolated by three panels. In this scene, the character representing the office manager is about to discover that one of his workers has dismantled one of the panels to expand the view.

Deskless Office

Office with no allocated desks, where each desk is equipped with a monitor and where computers and personal objects are removed each day at close of business. Employees store their belongings in personal lockers.

Digital Sweatshops

On-line companies which hire people to carry out poorly-paid routine tasks which can be done remotely on the employee's own computer.

Deskless Office

Google Central
London, 2012
Penson

Fourth floor plan

Dilbertian

Dilbert is a satirical character from a comic strip created by Scott Adams in 1989. He represents an engineer at a technological firm who has problems in the workplace. By extension, Dilbertian refers to any person who suffers the same working conditions as Dilbert.

Disaggregated Workforce

Also referred to as contingent, this is made up of non-permanent staff performing casual home-based activities for a company. The term was defined by Ryan Coonerty and Jeremy Neuner in their book *The Rise of the Naked Economy*, 2013.

Gamification

The introduction of gaming techniques and methods into business processes in order to increase productivity was an idea of Charles Coonradt who created the company The Game of Work in 1973. He subsequently went on to publish his experiences in his book *The Game of Work*, 1984.

Hierarchical Culture

This type of culture is related to large corporations and institutional structures. They value process standardization, efficient results and employee control. The decision-making process is assigned to those in senior management positions. Bruce M. Tharp, 2005.

| 45 | 9788469755358 | 45 |

WH: Aisle 15 Row: Bay 12
Bay: Shelf 4

ZBM.6ZQH

Title:	The Office On The Grass - The Evolution Of The Workplace
Cond:	Good
User:	bc_ravneetk
Station:	Lister 03
Date:	2025-01-16 17:04:18 (UTC)
Account:	Zoom Books Company
Orig Loc:	Aisle 15 Bay 12 Shelf 4
nSKU:	ZBM.6ZQH
vSKU:	ZBV.8469755358.G
Seq#:	45
unit_id:	25624347
width:	0.63 in
rank:	4,038,289

ZBV.8469755358.G

delist unit# 25624347

xxxxx

Dilbertian

Dilbert
Comic strip, 1989
Scott Adams

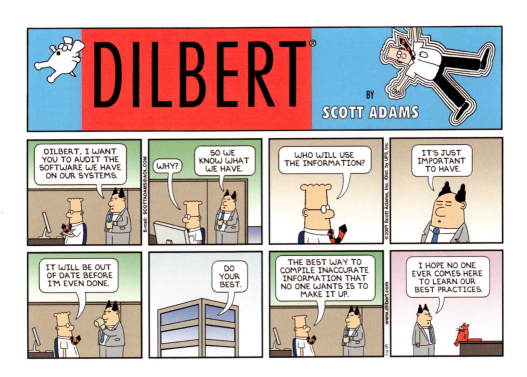

Huddle Room

Meetup spaces inside the office environment, with informal furniture, where employees can have 3- or 4-person conversations.

Informal Mentoring

Relationship built up between two people, whereby the older of the two listens, advises and trains the younger person, with no obligation or contract.

Mechanical Turk

Simple low-paid digital system for carrying out routine work which is done by people rather than machines as it requires a minimum level of human intelligence. Workers are casual and home-based.

Microworker

Worker carrying out small tasks for on-line companies. The worker chooses the hours and the workplace. As this work takes up only a few minutes of the working day, it is compatible with a full-time job.

Multi-generation Workforce

The following generations all co-exist in the current workplace: Babyboomers (born between 1940 and 1964), Generation X (1965-1980) and Millennium or Generation Y (1981-1995). Generation Z (1996-2010) is the next in line.

Huddle Room

Google Zurich
Hurlimann Areal, Zurich, 2008
Camenzind Evolution

A polar setting, complete with snow and penguins, surrounds these informal socializing and meeting spaces (huddlerooms) for three or four people which are divided off from the office with white string curtains which provide a certain degree of privacy.

Cisco Meraki
San Francisco, 2013
Studio O+A

In this office, there are spaces for concentrated activity, aimed either at private reflection or for working in small groups, which takes place in yurt-like constructions made from wooden structures and triangle-shaped elements filled with absorbent material.

People-centric Workspace

The term derives from people-centred development strategy, a movement aiming to empower communities and people against institutions. In terms of work organization, it reflects the will to improve the quality of the work space in accordance with employee needs rather than production requirements.

Reverse Mentoring

Relationship between two people in which the mentor is a young person, generally with less experience, who has stronger skills in a specific knowledge area. This often occurs when Generation Y members give Baby-boomer executives training in technological issues.

Sick Building Syndrome

Set of workplace-related symptoms in buildings with low-quality air, contamination from certain building materials, bad lighting and lack of appropriate noise insulation.

Sound Masking

Technique which involves adding sound frequencies to an open-plan office in an aim to mitigate the disturbing sensation resulting from conversations and background noise. Noise-cancelling speakers are used to suppress this noise.

People-centric Workspace

FiftyThree
New York, 2014
+ADD

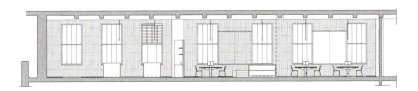

A bar counter with stools or armchairs which resemble those of a domestic living room are design resources to camouflage the corporate character of an office. Inserting unusual furnishings means other realities may be created within the work spaces such as leisure or household environments.

Swarm Work

Way of working which, unlike teamwork, is conducted by members who occasionally get together to perform a specific task, with no hierarchy and with no prior relationship between them and whose collaboration culminates when the task finishes. It is a way of working common in adhocracy which is also used in corporate firms.

Super-flexibility

Capacity of a large company to stay agile and versatile while also being robust and resistant, adopting features common to small enterprises in their operations.

Taylorist Office

Space based on the scientific organization of work, according to Frederick Winslow Taylor, 1911, who aimed to maximize productivity by using a process system based on the division of labour and time control.

Third Places

Places where administrative, creative or business tasks unrelated to the home (first place) or the traditional office (second place) are performed. Main features are informality, security, being open to the public and a good atmosphere. Examples of third spaces are: libraries, cafeterias, community centres, bookstores, parks... The term was described by Ray Oldenburg in his book *The Great Good Place*, 1989.

Third Places

The British Library at St Pancras
London, 1982-1999
Sir Colin St John Wilson and M. J. Long

These six people in the interior of a library have a complete workstation. The furniture consists of a desk chair with arms into which all their devices may be plugged and an independent desk which can easily be adapted to all their needs and adjustments. The lighting system is also personalized. The library provides them with a place to work within a concentrated quiet working environment.

Working desks located along the Library aisles

ACE Hotel. Shoreditch
London, 2013
Universal Design Studio

Lobby

Touchdown Space

In shared work spaces this is the most open area. It is used by people who are passing through or starting up their careers. They include the minimum services required to perform an activity: a counter with stools and Internet access.

Triple Bottom Line

Criterion assessing the success of a company from three viewpoints: financial results, social responsibility and respect for the environment. The term was first used by John Elkington in 1994.

Touchdown Space

DI_Telegraph
Moscow, 2014
Archiproba

This co-working company in Moscow has an area with three desks brought together for fourteen people with the basic layout of one workstation: chair, workspace and Internet connection. These occupy a free 7-metre high space in a large reclaimed office building.

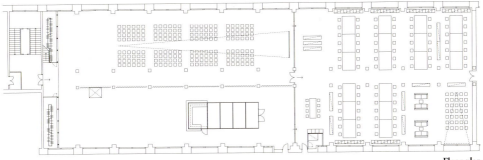

Floor plan

Vibe of Working

Feature of the work environment referring to that intangible part regarding comfort and sensations. This is the third attribute to be taken into consideration in collaborative work spaces, after location and infrastructure. The importance of this third feature was highlighted by Ryan Coonerty/Jeremy Neuner in their book *The Rise of the Naked Economy*, 2013.

Work Culture

Working practises specific to a given environment or location which may or should influence the design of the workplace.

Work Modes

Focusing, collaborating, learning and socializing. These are the four ways in which the knowledge worker operates according to the Gensler Workplace Survey, 2008.

Vibe of Working

LBi Offices
East London, 2008
Brinkworth

In the design for a workplace, the intangible elements are as important as the spatial layout or the choice of furniture. In the London HQ of this digital marketing company there are areas which are unrecognizable as workspaces yet which give off positive vibes which in turn spread to the whole office.

Timeline

Major innovations made in the office environment since its inception.

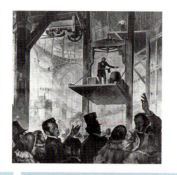

1857
PUBLIC ELEVATOR
Elisha Otis
New York

1873
TYPEWRITER
E. Remington and Sons
Ilion, N. Y.

Otis invented a braking element as a safety system for elevators which boosted public confidence. The first commercial elevator was installed in a large department store located at 490 Broadway. The elevator was a resource necessary to vertically connect the different storeys in the building and this led to the speculative development of the high-rise office.

In the last quarter of the 19th Century, Remington launched commercial production of the QWERTY-keyboard typewriter which was to become an office standard. The expansion period lasted slightly over a hundred years until the late 1980s when the word processor and the PC led to the end of mass use.

THE OFFICE ON THE GRASS

1876
TELEPHONE
Alexander Graham Bell

1885
STRUCTURAL STEEL FRAME
William Le Baron Jenney
Chicago

1902
AIR CONDITIONING
Willis Carrier
Brooklyn, N. Y.

The possibility of transmitting information over long distances enabled the administration space to become separate from the production space. The office building typology was born.

The Home Insurance Building is considered to be the first high-rise building constructed using steel columns and beams. It was the headquarters of an insurance company. The aim of the design was for bright open-plan spaces. The brickwork modular openings in the facades are the precursor of the glass-steel curtain wall. The steel frame optimized use and distribution of the interior space due to a good ratio between the net floor area and the gross floor area.

The first central air conditioning system was installed in a Brooklyn printer's to control the humidity of the paper during the printing process. Four years later Carrier was to patent the Apparatus for Treating Air that brought the onset of air conditioning systems which would later be installed in most modern office buildings.

TIMELINE

1912
GLASS SKYLIGHT ATRIUM
Otto Wagner
Vienna

1930-1939
THE TAYLORIST URBAN COMPLEX
Raymond Hood
New York

1937
TASK-ORIENTED FURNITURE
Frank Lloyd Wright
Metal Office Furniture Co./ Steelcase

The religious character of the glass vault afforded to the atrium was a solution repeated later in many office buildings due to its overwhelming transparency. Daylight penetrates the operations room of this bank and reduces consumption of artificial lighting. Wright recreated this atmosphere nearly three decades later in the building for Johnson Wax in Racine.

The Rockefeller Center represents the Taylorist model office, based on space optimization by stacking long floor plans with a central vertical circulation core. The organization of workstations into rows is still dependent on proximity to a natural light source. It was the first urban development in the world to include offices, retail, leisure and restaurants in one single complex.

This series of furniture is the basis of the modern workstation. A triple-level desk with a three-legged chair on wheels (which initially had some stability issues). This was designed by Wright for the Great Workroom in the Johnson Wax Building.

THE OFFICE ON THE GRASS

1939
THE GREAT WORKROOM
Frank Lloyd Wright
Racine, Wi.

1943
THE KNOLL PLANNING UNIT
Florence Knoll
New York

1950
MECHANICAL PLANT
W. K. Harrison, Le Corbusier,
O. Niemeyer and others
New York

In the Great Workroom of the Johnson Wax administration building there is no sensation of being enclosed. The bright interior space has no walls and divisions and employees are distributed over a hierarchy-free floor within a forest of mushroom-shaped columns.

Between the 1940s and the 1960s Florence Knoll (maiden name Schust) was highly influential in the interior design of American corporate buildings due to her view of the office as a whole in accordance with the architectural ideas of the German masters (Mies van der Rohe, Walter Gropius and Marcel Breuer) of the Bauhaus.

The United Nations Secretariat tower uses fragmentation of installations by floors to avoid any hindrance of the power of the machinery due to the excessive length of the service shafts in high-rise buildings. In the thirty-nine storey Secretariat building, four floors, as well as the roof, are occupied solely by air conditioning systems.

TIMELINE

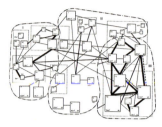  

1956
BÜROLANDSCHAFT
Quickborner Team:
Wolfgang and Eberhard Schnelle
Hamburg

1957
EXTENSIVE AMENITIES
SOM (Skidmore, Owings and Merrill) and Knoll
Bloomfield, Ct.

1957
CLEAR-SPAN CONSTRUCTION
SOM (Skidmore, Owings and Merrill)
Chicago

This is an evolution of the Taylorist office towards greater interaction among the staff occupying a workplace. The layout of the landscape office takes a stance against hierarchical culture and adopts a more egalitarian, flexible and organic distribution. Vegetation is incorporated to provide divisions and to increase privacy in each workstation.

The Connecticut General Life Insurance Company head office provided its employees with countless amenities to make this quiet workplace in the Connecticut countryside more appealing. There were swimming pools, board games, lending library, cleaning services, food, bowling alleys, sports courts, a bar and a cafeteria selling affordable food, as well as an auditorium for four hundred people.

The Inland Steel Building is supported by seven exterior columns at each of the longest sides of the facade. The interior is open-plan and free of any obstacles. There are no structural support elements within the perimeter. The circulation core, with its six elevators, service elevator and two staircases, is also a tower which is separate from the office storeys. It was renovated in 2008.

THE OFFICE ON THE GRASS

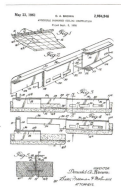

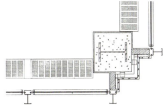

1958
ACCESSIBLE SUSPENDED CEILING
Donald A. Brown
Westlake, Oh.

1958
CURTAIN-WALL
Mies van der Rohe
New York

1961
THE AUTONOMOUS OFFICE
SOM (Skidmore, Owings and Merrill)
New York

The invention of the accessible ceiling facilitated quick and easy access to the service installations running below the slab without having to perform expensive demolition and reconstruction work. This, along with modular fluorescent lighting which consumes less than incandescent lighting, was and still is a common solution for the upper surface of the contemporary office.

The elegant structure of the facade of the Seagram Building is visible from the exterior. The bronze I-beams of the curtain wall (which required cleaning with lemon oil) established a model envelope which was to be recreated in a more awkward fashion in several corporate buildings. The would-be replicas never quite managed to attain either the level of refinement of this glass box or its iconic power as a black monolith.

The Chase Manhattan Bank Building is the paradigm of the office of a great American company. The workstation becomes autonomous in terms of light and ventilation due to the mass use of fluorescent lighting and air conditioning and the floor plan has a depth which is not determined by a maximum distance to the facade.

TIMELINE

1964
ACTION OFFICE FURNITURE SYSTEM
Robert Propst
Herman Miller, Inc.
Ann Arbor, Mi.

1968
GREEN ATRIUM
Kevin Roche/John Dinkeloo
New York

1973
THE WORKERS' VILLAGE
Herman Hertzberger
Apeldoorn

Although initially Action Office might be considered to be the precursor of the cubicle farm, the designer Robert Propst was against closing off employees with office furniture and subsequent system solutions were closer to the open-plan office. The second version of the system, dating from 1968, already foresaw vertical mobility at the workstation between sit/stand positions.

The main lobby of the Ford Foundation spreads the visual relationship between offices out to the whole of the building, establishing contact between employees and the vegetation growing on lower levels and extending the workplace out into the nearby urban environment.

The Centraal Beheer insurance company is a sort of 'workers' village' designed such that staff 'would have the feeling of being part of a working community without being lost in the crowd. Each individual is empowered to act on their own work space and maintain their privacy as against previous models where corporate efficiency, control and productivity prevailed.

THE OFFICE ON THE GRASS

1985
EXTERIOR SERVICE TOWERS
Richard Rogers Partnership
London

1987
INNER STREET
Niels Torp
Stockholm

1989
WORLD WIDE WEB
Tim Berners-Lee
Geneva

In the Lloyd's of London Building the service areas leave the central space free and are joined to the perimeter as add-ons to the prismatic volume of the offices. This separation of the more technical components of the building ensures greater accessibility from the exterior and means they can be replaced more easily in the event of their becoming obsolete.

In the SAS headquarters, Niels Torp follows the scheme of an inner street shrouded in vegetation as a central spine serving several buildings. The street is staggered and leads down to a lake at the end. It is a social space for company employees to socialize and there is also a café and an auditorium. Included in the route, in a central position, is a swimming pool and a sports hall to underline that maintaining a healthy body is a corporate concern.

The telegraph and the telephone are two communication devices which in their day revolutionized long-distance data transmission. The web was a leap forward in global communications due to its potential for real-time data exchange. In the business world, the internet has opened up the office and distributed it out into unexpected places. The working schedule has stretched and business relationships have spilled out onto social media with unlimited connectivity.

TIMELINE

1989
THE OUT-OF-TOWN BUSINESS PARK
Foster + Partners
Uxbridge

1991
THE ICONIC OFFICE
Frank Gehry/Claes Oldenburg, Coosje van Bruggen
Los Angeles

1998
ADVERTISING CITY
CWA (Clive Wilkinson Architects)
Los Angeles

Stockley Park was one of the first out-of-town business parks in the United Kingdom. Designed in the 1980s, it fled the high real estate prices of central London and settled in a location with good transport links, between the M4 and M25 motorways and close to Heathrow Airport. These low-rise buildings, which enjoy pleasant vistas and are surrounded by landscaped gardens, compete against the centrality of offices in the City.

This building designed by Gehry for the Chiat Day advertising agency fittingly embraces the philosophy of media firms due to its highly iconic content identifiable in three very different constructions: a boat, a tree and a pair of oversized binoculars (Oldenburg). Google took over the Chiat/Day Building in 2011 to set up its Venice office and to take advantage of the strong brand image.

When CWA built the interior of the TBWA/Chiat/Day advertising agency, it was called Advertising City due to its strong urban character and the interior advertising hoardings. It included a main street, a large central park, a basketball court and a vast quantity of meetup spaces inside tents for specific projects, something CWA would repeat six years later in the Googleplex.

THE OFFICE ON THE GRASS

1998
THE FUN OFFICE
FAT: Sam Jacob, Sean Griffiths, Charles Holland
Amsterdam

2001
EAR-CHAIR
Studio Makkink&Bey
Tilburg

2004
THE CAMPUS COMMUNITY COMPLEX
CWA/DEGW/William McDonough
Mountain View, Ca.

The Kessels Kramer advertising agency, located in an old church, had a surreal design containing a Russian wooden fort, a lifeguard tower, garden sheds, pieces of football pitches and a picnic table. All these elements are orchestrated in an aim to subvert the conventional workplace and turn the office into a fun place.

The concept of Activity Based Working is based on flexible workstations which reduce the numbers of desks and offices in a workplace. It was applied by Erik Veldhoen in the head office of the insurance company Interpolis. The building, designed by Bonnema Architechten, was commenced in 1993 and the last items of furniture were installed ten years later. The *pièce-de-résistance* is the Ear-chair by Jurgen Bey, initially designed for the reception area. This chair creates privacy to enable focus while also facilitating teamwork in an open room.

Googleplex was purchased from Silicon Graphics in 2003 and later converted to a corporate campus boasting good interconnectivity with outdoor spaces such as the sports areas, large communal lawns, gardens and ponds. The buildings are structured like a college campus as the work areas combine with research and learning, both essential resources to a creative company.

TIMELINE

2005
FIRST OFFICIAL COWORKING SPACE
Brad Neuberg
San Francisco

2013
THE OFFICE WITHOUT MECHANICALS
Baumschlager Eberle
Lustenau

2017
PASTORAL SIMPLICITY
Foster and Partners/Arup Associates
Cupertino, Ca.

SpiralMuse, Home of Wellbeing, was the first recognized coworking space for freelancers and writers. It was active for one year and later was converted to the Hat Factory which also no longer exists. There were eight tables, communal eating areas and meditation and massage rooms. Located in a refurbished Victorian house in San Francisco, it looked more like a Bed&Breakfast than a workplace. The number of coworkers was limited to five persons.

This office building has no HVAC system. The energy flow is manually-controlled. There is a cavity wall structure with 36 centimetre. The interior layer provides high compressive strength and the outer layer insulation. In summer the vents are opened providing natural ventilation. This is a reaction to the Modernist concept of buildings acting as power stations.

In Apple headquarters, Cupertino, designed for 13,000 employees, Foster and Partners combine Arup's previous experiments using environmentally-friendly ideas of the self-sufficient building with a sophisticated, simple and robust design integrated into the Santa Clara countryside. It is pastoral simplicity, taken in part from the Apple philosophy, located in the fruit groves of California, the countryside where Steve Jobs grew up, with the proportion of the Stanford campus buildings.

Bibliography

Aureli, Pier Vittorio. "The Barest Form in which Architecture Can Exist: Some Notes on Ludwig Hilberseimer's Proposal for the Chicago Tribune Building."
The City as a Project, 2011

Bauman, Zygmunt. *The Liquid Modernity*. Polity Press, 2000.

Bollier, David. *The future of work: what it means for individuals, business, markets and governments*. The Aspen Institute, 2011.

Coonerty, Ryan and Neuner, Jeremy. *The rise of the naked economy: how to benefit from the changing workplace*.
Palgrave Macmillan, 2013.

CoreNet: Office space per workers shrinks to 150 sf.
Building Design + Construction, 2013.

Drucker, Peter F. *Managing in the next society*. Griffin, 1994.

Duffy, Francis. *Work and the City*. Black Dog Architecture, 2008.

Duffy, Francis and Tanis, Jack. 'A vision of the new workplace'. T*he International Development Research Council's Journal*, 1993.
Eggers, Dave. *The Circle*. Knopf. Mcsweeney Books, 2013.

Florida, Richard. *The great reset: how the post-crash economy will change the way we live and work*. Harper Business, 2011.

Foucault, Michel. "Of other spaces, Heterotopias". *Architecture, Mouvement, Continuité* 5 (1984): 46-49

Gensler. 2013 US Workplace Survey. Key Findings.

Gensler. It's the Economy. Design Forecast, 2013

Heerwagen, Judith H. Design, *Productivity and Well Being: What Are the Links?* March 12-14, 1998.

Heerwagen, Judith H. "Green Buildings, Organizational Success, and Occupant Productivity". *Building Research and Information*, Vol. 28 (5), 2000.

Hipple, Steven F. "About 1 in 9 workers was self-employed in 2009". Self-employment in the United States. *Monthly Labor Review*. September 2010.

Horowitz, Sara. "What is New Mutualism?" *Freelancers Union*, 2013

Horowitz, Sara and Poynter, Sciarra. *The freelancer's Bible: everything you need to know to have the career of your dreams-on your terms*. Workman Publishing Company, 2012.

Jacob, Sam. 'Offices designed as fun palaces are fundamentally sinister'. *Dezeen magazine*. 28 February 2013

Jung, Carl. *The psychology of the child archetype. The special phenomenology of the child archetype. The invincibility of the child.* Princeton University Press, 1968.

Yves Béhar/fuseproject. Living Office. Solutions. Products. Herman Miller. 2013.

Louie, Elaine. "Table Manners at Work" Home&Garden. *The New York Times*. February, 2014.

Marmot, Alexi. *Office space planning: designing for tomorrow's workplace*. McGraw-Hill Professional, 2000.

Myerson, Jeremy / Bichard, Jo-Anne/ Erlich, Alma. *New Demographics New Workspace*. Office Design for the Changing Workforce. Gower, 2010.

Oldenburg, Ray. *The great good place: cafés, coffee shops, bookstores, bars, hair salons, and other hangouts at the heart of a community*. Da Capo Pr., 1999.

Ouroussoff, Nicolai. "A work through the looking glass" *Los Angeles Times*. January 31, 1999.

Penenberg, Adam L. *Play at Work. How games inspire breakthrough thinking*. Piatkus, 2013.

Pew Research Center. *Millennials. A portrait of Generation Next. Confident. Connected. Open to Change.* 2010.

Saval, Nikil. *Cubed. A Secret History of the Workplace*. Doubleday, 2014.

Slim, Pamela. *Escape from cubicle nation: from corporate prisoner to thriving entrepreneur*. Berkley, 2009.

Stone, Philip J. and Luchetti, Robert. "Your office is where you are". *Harvard Business Review*, 1985.

Stringer, Leigh. World's largest workplace survey. *Using Facebook to transform the workplace*. HOK. 2012.

Thomas, Claire. "Google was cubicle land when we started designing offices for them". *Dezeen magazine*. March 2014.

US General Services Administration. Sound matters: how to achieve acoustic comfort in the contemporary office. GSA Public Buildings Service, 2011.

van Meel, Juriaan. *The european office: office design and national context*.
010 Publishers, 2000.

White, Martha C. "Start-up chic goes corporate, as couches replace desks". Commercial. *The New York Times*. 2013.

Wilkinson, Clive. "Designing spaces for new ways of working". *Designboom*. May 2014.

a+t

FORM&DATA
Collective Housing Projects:
An Anatomical Review
a+t research group
ISBN 978-84-608-1485-6 2016. English/Spanish edition

WHY DENSITY?
Debunking the myth of the cubic watermelon
a+t research group
ISBN 978-84-606-5751-4 2015. English/Spanish edition

10 STORIES OF COLLECTIVE HOUSING
Graphical analysis of inspiring masterpieces
a+t research group
ISBN 978-84-616-4136-9 2013. English edition
(También disponible edición en Español)

DENSITY IS HOME
Housing by a+t research group
ISBN 978-84-615-1237-9 2011. English/Spanish edition

NEXT
Collective Housing in progress
ISBN 978-84-613-8676-5 2010. English/Spanish edition

HoCo
Density Housing Construction & Costs
ISBN 978-84-613-3080-5 2009. English/Spanish edition

DENSITY PROJECTS
36 new concepts on collective housing
ISBN 978-84-612-1335-1 2007.
English/Spanish (only online version)

DBOOK
Digital Files
ISBN 978-84-611-5900-0 2007.
English/Spanish (only digital edition)

DENSITY. CONDENSED EDITION
New collective housing
ISBN 84-611-1203-2 2006.
English/Spanish (only online version)

THIS IS HYBRID
An analysis of mixed-use buildings
a+t research group
ISBN 978-84-616-6237-1 2014. English/Spanish edition

THE PUBLIC CHANCE
New urban landscapes
ISBN 978-84-612-4488-1 2008. English/Spanish edition

RASHOMON
La triple verdad de la arquitectura
ISBN 978-84-615-4944-3 2011. Spanish edition